SPECTRUM

4

A Communicative Course in English

Diane Warshawsky
with *Donald R. H. Byrd*

Donald R. H. Byrd *Project Director*

Anna Veltfort *Art Director*

PRENTICE HALL REGENTS
Upper Saddle River, NJ 07458

Library of Congress has cataloged the full edition of this title as follows
Warshawsky, Diane.
    Spectrum 4, a communicative course in English/ Diane Warshawsky
    with Donald R.H. Byrd.
       p.   cm.
       ISBN 0-13-830159-X (full)
    1. English language—textbooks for foreign speakers.   I. Byrd
Donald R.H. Byrd II. Title.   III. Title: Spectrum four.
PE1128.W364 1994   9340685
428.2'4—dc20   CIP

ISBN (4A)   0-13-832775-0   ISBN (4B)   0-13-832791-2

Project Manager: Nancy L. Leonhardt
Manager of Development Services: Louisa B. Hellegers
Editorial Consultant: Larry Anger
Development Editors: Stephanie I. Karras, D. Andrew Gitzy
Audio Development Editor: D. Andrew Gitzy
Assistants to the Editors: Sylvia P. Bloch, Jennifer Fader

Director of Production and Manufacturing: David Riccardi
Editorial Production/Design Manager: Dominick Mosco
Production Editor and Compositor: Christine McLaughlin Mann
Page Composition: Ken Liao
Electronic Production Coordinator: Molly Pike Riccardi
Production Coordinator: Ray Keating
Production Assistant: Wanda España

Cover Design Coordinator: Marianne Frasco
Cover Design: Roberto de Vicq
Electronic Art: Todd Ware

Interior Concept and Page-by-Page Design: Anna Veltfort

Audio Program Producer: Paul Ruben Productions

 © 1995 by Prentice Hall Regents
Prentice-Hall, Inc.
Simon & Schuster/A Viacom Company
Upper Saddle River, New Jersey 07458

Printed in the United States of America

10 9 8 7 6 5

ISBN 0-13-830159-X

Printed on Recycled Paper

Prentice Hall International (UK) Limited, *London*
Prentice Hall of Australia Pty. Limited, *Sydney*
Prentice Hall Canada, Inc., *Toronto*
Prentice Hall Hispanoamericana, S.A., *Mexico*
Prentice Hall of India Private Limited, *New Delhi*
Prentice Hall of Japan, Inc., *Tokyo*
Simon & Schuster Asia Pte. Ltd., *Singapore*
Editora Prentice Hall do Brasil, Ltda., *Rio de Janeiro*

INTRODUCTION

Welcome to the new edition of *Spectrum! Spectrum 4* represents the fourth level of a six-level course designed for adolescent and adult learners of English. The student book, workbook, and audio program for each level provide practice in all four communication skills, with a special focus on listening and speaking. Levels 1 and 2 are appropriate for beginning students and "false" beginners. Levels 3 and 4 are intended for intermediate classes, and 5 and 6 for advanced learners of English. The first four levels are offered in split editions — 1A, 1B, 2A, 2B, 3A, 3B, 4A, and 4B. The student books, workbooks, audio programs, and teacher's editions for levels 1 to 4 are also available in full editions.

Spectrum is a "communicative" course in English, based on the idea that communication is not merely an end-product of language study, but rather the very process through which a new language is acquired. *Spectrum* involves students in this process from the very beginning by providing them with useful, natural English along with opportunities to discuss topics of personal interest and to communicate their own thoughts, feelings, and ideas.

In *Spectrum*, comprehension is considered the starting point for communication. The student books thus emphasize the importance of comprehension, both as a useful skill and as a natural means of acquiring a language. Students begin each unit by listening to and reading conversations that provide rich input for language learning. Accompanying activities enhance comprehension and give students time to absorb new vocabulary and structures. Throughout the unit students encounter readings and dialogues containing structures and expressions not formally introduced until later units or levels. The goal is to provide students with a continuous stream of input that challenges their current knowledge of English, thereby allowing them to progress naturally to a higher level of competence.

Spectrum emphasizes interaction as another vital step in language acquisition. Interaction begins with simple communication tasks that motivate students to use the same structure a number of times as they exchange real information about themselves and other topics. This focused practice builds confidence and fluency and prepares students for more open-ended activities involving role playing, discussion, and problem solving. These activities give students control of the interaction and enable them to develop strategies for expressing themselves and negotiating meaning in an English-speaking environment.

The *Spectrum* syllabus is organized around functions and structures practiced in thematic lessons. Both functions and structures are carefully graded according to level of difficulty, and usefulness. Structures are presented in clear paradigms with informative usage notes. Thematic lessons provide interesting topics for interaction and a meaningful vehicle for introducing vocabulary.

This student book consists of fourteen units, each divided into one- and two-page lessons. Each unit begins with a preview page that outlines the functions/themes, language, and forms (grammar) in the unit. A preview activity prepares students to understand the cultural material in the conversations that begin each unit and gives them the opportunity to contribute their own background knowledge. The first lesson in each unit presents a series of realistic conversations, providing input for comprehension and language acquisition. New functions and structures are then practiced through interactive tasks in several thematic lessons. A one-page, fully illustrated comprehension lesson provides further input in the form of a dialogue and listening exercise both related to the storyline for the level. The next one-page lesson provides pronunciation practice and includes discussion or role-playing activities that draw on students' personal experience. The final lesson of the unit presents realistic documents such as historical texts and news articles for reading comprehension practice. There are review lessons after units 4, 7, 11, and 14. An accompanying workbook, audio cassette program, and teacher's edition are available.

For the preparation of the new edition, Prentice Hall Regents would like to thank the following long-time users of Spectrum, whose insights and suggestions have helped to shape the content and format of the new edition: Motofumi Aramaki, Sony Language Laboratory, Tokyo, Japan; Associacão Cultural Brasil-Estados Unidos (ACBEU), Salvador-Bahia, Brazil; AUA Language Center, Bangkok, Thailand, Thomas J. Kral and faculty; Pedro I. Cohen, Professor Emeritus of English, Linguistics, and Education, Universidad de Panamá; ELSI Taiwan Language Schools, Taipei, Taiwan, Kenneth Hou and faculty; James Hale, Sundai ELS, Tokyo, Japan; Impact, Santiago, Chile; Instituto Brasil-Estados Unidos (IBEU), Rio de Janeiro, Brazil; Instituto Brasil-Estados Unidos No Ceará (IBEU-CE), Fortaleza, Brazil; Instituto Chileno Norteamericano de Cultura, Santiago, Chile; Instituto Cultural Argentino Norteamericano (ICANA), Buenos Aires, Argentina; Christopher M. Knott, Chris English Masters Schools, Kyoto, Japan; The Language Training and Testing Center, Taipei, Taiwan, Anthony Y. T. Wu and faculty; Lutheran Language Institute, Tokyo, Japan; Network Cultura, Ensino e Livraria Ltda, São Paulo, Brazil; Seven Language and Culture, São Paulo, Brazil.

S E Q U E N C E

LANGUAGE	FORMS	SKILLS
How was it? It was one of the nicest vacations I've ever taken. I'm not working at the camera store anymore. You aren't?/You're not? Soccer is a really exciting game, isn't it? Yes, it really is. To tell you the truth, I don't think it's *that* exciting. Soccer isn't a very exciting game, is it? No, it really isn't. Actually, I think it's *very* exciting. You're from Tokyo, aren't you?	The superlative of adjectives with the present perfect Rejoinders showing interest or surprise Tag questions	Listen for opinions about vacations Listen to surprising or interesting statements Listen to the intonation of rejoinders Read a short historical text Write an article about an interesting place (workbook)
How do you like living here? I love it. I miss being near my family. Would you like to study for the test now, or would you rather take it easy? I'd just as soon take it easy. It doesn't matter to me. I'm not used to getting up early. I'm used to eating a big breakfast. I'm so tired. It's such a long trip. I'm not used to so much work. I'm not used to so many people. I'm looking forward to going to the play tonight. You must be good at learning languages. I have a hard time learning languages.	*Be used to* *So* vs. *such* Gerunds	Listen for likes and dislikes Listen to people talk about their habits Listen to people complain Listen to the emphasis of statements with *so* and *such* Read an interview Write a letter (workbook)
Who's it by? It was written by Shakespeare. Dostoyevsky wrote *War and Peace*, didn't he? No, *War and Peace* was written by Tolstoy. I'm not sure who wrote it. The Pyramids at Giza were built around 2500 B.C. My wife was just promoted to manager. That's really good news. My husband was laid off a couple of weeks ago. I'm sorry to hear that. I need someone to take care of my daughter. What kind of person are you looking for? Someone who's good with children. Do you know of anyone who baby-sits and can cook? I have a friend whose son likes to baby-sit. What's it about? It's about a group of Chinese women who live in San Francisco.	The passive in the past tense The passive without an agent Relative clauses with *who* and *whose*	Listen to people talk about books, movies, and music Listen for job requirements Listen to the intonation of statements and questions Read two book jackets Write a movie or book review (workbook)
Is everybody here? Everyone but Ana (is). Everyone's here except Ana. What should we have for dinner? Anything is fine with me. Anything but pizza. Actually, I don't want to have anything. I'm not hungry. He said not to wait for him. She said to wait for her. How does Wednesday at ten sound? I'm busy all day. I'm busy the whole week. I work every Wednesday. I won't be able to make it. I might not be able to make it. I wish I'd known earlier. Do you happen to know John's phone number? Not offhand, but I can look it up for you in my address book.	Indefinite compounds with *except* and *but* *The whole*, *all*, and *every* with time expressions	Listen to people make plans Listen to people make a decision Listen to people take messages Listen to people ask for information Listen to the intonation of statements and questions Read a magazine article Respond to a formal invitation (workbook)
Review	Review	Review

LANGUAGE	FORMS	SKILLS

We went camping in the mountains last week. During the trip, we had a flat tire.
While we were at the concert, someone broke into our house.
Now, what was I saying? You were telling me that during your trip. . .
I was born in Singapore. I grew up in Hong Kong. I lived there for seventeen
  years.
If I had more time, I'd travel. Where would you go? I think I'd go to Africa.
What would you do if no one answered the phone?
What delicious cheese! Where is it made? It's made in Switzerland.
This building was built in 1776.
Cars are manufactured in Japan.
Coffee is grown in Brazil.
	While vs. *during*
	Contrary-to-fact
	  conditionals
	The passive in the
	  present and past
		Listen to people talk about
		  their vacation
		Listen to people talk about
		  their lives
		Listen to the intonation of
		  conditional sentences
		Read a short historical text
		Write responses for a
		  newspaper interview
		  (workbook)

Can I get you anything while I'm out? Do you think you might go by a post
  office? I could.
What would you like? Could you have them weigh this package?
I'd like to have this film developed.
He'd like to have them develop this film.
Would you mind mailing some letters? No, not at all.
Could you get me a book of first-class stamps? Sure.
I might as well get a tie.
	The causative *have*
	Noun compounds
		Listen to people ask favors
		Listen to people talk about
		  shopping
		Listen to the intonation of
		  statements with the
		  causative *have*
		Read a magazine article
		Write a letter of complaint
		  about something you
		  bought (workbook)

I was reading in bed when I heard footsteps downstairs.
He started up the stairs while I was talking on the phone.
It was a cold winter night. It was after midnight when I left the party . . .
I'm sorry if I frightened you. Oh, that's O.K. Don't worry about it.
Haven't we met somewhere before? Yes, I think we met in Santiago last year.
Why doesn't he write more often? He hates to write letters.
Where did you say you lived? At 26 Larchmount Terrace.
	The simple past vs.
	  the past continuous
	  with *when* and *while*
	Negative questions
		Listen to a frightening story
		Listen to the intonation of
		  information questions
		Read a magazine article
		Write an ending to a story
		  (workbook)

Review	Review	Review

I'm sorry to let you down, but I can't go to the concert tonight. I have too much
  work to do. That's O.K. I understand.
You'd better give it to her. You'd better not interrupt her.
Would you mind if I opened the window? Not at all. Go right ahead.
  Well . . . I'd rather you didn't.
I'd really appreciate it if you could help me print out my report. I think I can.
  I wish I could, but I have to work.
I really appreciate your helping me. I'm happy to do it. I'm sure you'd do
  the same for me.
What time are we supposed to meet Carla and Rob? At six . . .
	Infinitives after direct
	  objects
	Had better and *had
	  better not*
	Be supposed to
		Listen for an excuse
		Listen to someone give
		  advice
		Listen to someone ask
		  favors
		Listen to the intonation of
		  statements
		Take a quiz
		Write a response to a memo
		  (workbook)

Are you going to go camping this weekend? If it stops raining. / Not unless it
  stops raining. / Not if it doesn't stop raining.
You're not supposed to park here unless you have a permit.
You don't have to eat the hamburgers.
Did you hurt yourself? Yes. I have this sharp pain between my shoulders, and
  I think I might have sprained my ankle. I'd better call an ambulance.
She told me not to come over.
He told me to take it easy and not to lift anything heavy.
	If vs. *unless*
	Be supposed to vs.
	  have to in negative
	  statements
	Reported speech with
	  imperatives
		Listen to vacation plans
		Listen for a message
		Listen to vowel and
		  consonant reduction and
		  blending in *supposed to*
		  and *have to*
		Read a magazine article
		Write directions (workbook)

LANGUAGE	FORMS	SKILLS
I haven't been getting much sleep lately. If I were you, I'd take some time off. Have you been getting enough exercise? I'm in a really bad mood. I feel like quitting my job. I know how that is. I've felt like that myself. You'd better not push yourself too hard, or you'll be exhausted. Thanks for the advice. Don't mention it.	The present perfect continuous *Had better* and *had better not* Reflexive pronouns	Listen for advice Listen for people's moods Listen for a problem Listen to statements with reflexive pronouns Read a magazine article Write a letter (workbook)
I haven't seen you in ages. I've been meaning to call you, but I've been so busy. What have you been doing lately? I haven't been doing much of anything. I've been playing a lot of tennis. In fact, I've played three nights this week. Do you want to play tennis sometime? Sure. If I have time next week, I'll give you a call. If I had more money, I'd travel around the world. Really? If I had more money I'd try to save it. I'd fit into this suit if I lost a few pounds. I'm always late to work. If you got up earlier, you wouldn't be late.	The present perfect continuous vs. the present perfect Conditional sentences	Listen for what people have been doing Listen to people talk about their wishes Listen to vowel and consonant reduction and blending with *have* and *been* Analyze a song Write a letter (workbook)
Review	Review	Review
Do you know if there's a bank around here? I wonder if they exchange currency. Could you tell me if there are any inexpensive tours? I thought you were Mexican. I *am* Mexican. No, I'm Spanish. Have you ever had *paella*? Yes, I have. I thought it was delicious. No, I haven't. What is it? It's a rice dish made with seafood, chicken, and spices. It's cooked slowly in a large pan. It's too hot to go for a walk. / I don't have enough energy to go for a walk.	Embedded yes-no questions Sequence of tenses *Too . . . to* and *not . . . enough . . . to*	Listen for locations Listen to someone ask for travel information Listen to the emphasis of statements with *am* and *do* Read a magazine article Write a review (workbook)
Could I see that shirt, please? Which one? The plaid one. What's this blouse made of? It's made of silk. / It's 100 percent silk. I'm looking for a gift for my sister-in-law, but I'm not sure what to get her. Do you know if she has any hobbies? / Do you know what her hobbies are? What if he doesn't like it? Oh, I'm sure he will. Doesn't your sweater have a hole in it? I guess I should have looked it over more carefully. He should have tried them on in the store.	Embedded questions: yes-no questions vs. information questions *Should have*	Listen to descriptions of clothing Listen to people talk about their regrets Listen to vowel and consonant reduction and blending in *should have* and *shouldn't have* Read a short story Write a letter (workbook)
I wonder what's keeping Ed. He may/might have gotten lost. He may/might not have understood your directions. Do you think Ed got lost? Oh, I doubt it. He must not have written down the time. They may have gotten stuck in traffic. They might have left the house late. They must have had an accident. You were supposed to be here at noon. The bus broke down, so I had to walk. Did you tell him (that) I had an appointment at 3:30? Yes, and he said (that) he'd meet us for lunch at 2:00.	*May have*, *might have*, and *must have* *Be supposed to* vs. *have to* in the past Direct and reported speech	Listen to possibilities Listen and make a conclusion Listen for phone messages Listen to vowel and consonant reduction and blending in *must have*, *might have*, *may have*, and *should have* Read a magazine article Write a letter (workbook)
Review	Review	Review

PREVIEW

FUNCTIONS/THEMES	LANGUAGE	FORMS
Ask for and give an opinion	How was it? It was one of the nicest vacations I've ever taken.	The superlative of adjectives with the present perfect
Express surprise	I'm not working at the camera store anymore. You aren't?/You're not?	Rejoinders showing interest or surprise
Give an opinion Agree or disagree with an opinion	Soccer is a really exciting game, isn't it? Yes, it really is. To tell you the truth, I don't think it's that exciting. Soccer isn't a very exciting game, is it? No, it really isn't. Actually, I think it's *very* exciting.	Tag questions
Confirm information	You're from Tokyo, aren't you?	

Preview the conversations.

[handwritten notes:]
fascinate (ˈæsɪ)
озаровивать
get used to = used to
привыкать

[handwritten margin note:]
вносить
неуд

Hi, everyone!
    Peru is such a fascinating country. We spent the first week with Pablo's family, getting used to the altitude, and then a few days hiking in the Andes. The scenery is beautiful! Now we're back in Cuzco again, and our feet are getting the vacation they need. We miss you all very much!
            Love,
            Pablo and Sue

The Stone Family
225 Pine St.
Berkeley, CA 94703
U.S.A.

Read the postcard. Then work with a partner and talk about someplace you've gone or something you've done recently.

1. Find out if your partner enjoyed the activity.
2. Tell your partner your opinion of what you did.

1. Did you do anything special over the summer?

Some people who live in Berkeley, California, are catching up on what their friends have been doing.

A

Anita Rivera Carol! Hi!

Carol Thomas Hi, Anita! How are you?

Anita Just fine, thanks. What's new?

Carol Nothing much. What's new with you?

Anita Well, I'm not working at the bank anymore.

Carol You aren't?

Anita No. I've decided to go back to school to get my master's degree in economics.

Carol That's great! Listen, I've really got to run, but I'd like to hear more about your plans. We'll have to get together soon.

Anita Yes, we really should.

B

Lou Miller Did you do anything special over the summer?

Sue Romero We visited Pablo's family in Peru.

Lou You did? How was it?

Sue Wonderful! It was one of the nicest vacations we've ever taken. You've never been to Peru, have you?

Lou No, but I've always wanted to go. I hear the scenery is beautiful.

Figure it out

1. Listen to the conversations and choose the correct answers.

1. a. Anita and Carol see each other every day.
   - √ b. Anita and Carol haven't seen each other for a while.

2. √ a. Anita used to work at a bank.
   - b. Anita wants to work at a bank.

3. a. √ Anita and Carol make plans to get together.
   - b. Anita and Carol don't make any plans.

4. a. Lou enjoyed the scenery in Peru.
   - √ b. Lou would like to go to Peru.

5. √ a. Ken, Hiro, and Mary didn't agree about the Clancy book.
   - b. Ken, Hiro, and Mary all liked the Clancy book a lot.

C

Ken Parker Did you read any good books over the summer?

Hiro Ota As a matter of fact, I read a couple of thrillers by Tom Clancy.

Ken Oh, I've read Clancy's latest book, the one that just came out as a movie.

Hiro You have? That's the one I'm reading now.

Mary Collins I've read it, too. It's exciting, isn't it?

Hiro It really is.

Ken I thought it was O.K., but to tell you the truth, I didn't think it was *that* exciting.

Soon Kim Listen, I hate to break this up, but I've got to teach in fifteen minutes.

Ken I've got to get back to the office myself.

Hiro We'll have to do this again sometime.

Soon Yes, it's been fun.

matter of fact = smth that is really true. that can be proved.

1) affirmative, negative.
2)

2. Find another way to say it.

1. What did you think of it? *How was it?*
2. I think it's exciting, don't you? *It's exciting, isn't it?*
3. I agree that it's exciting. *It really is*
4. I'm surprised you're not. *You aren't!*
5. It was a great vacation. *It was one of the nicest*
6. I have to go now. *I've got to run.*
I've got to get back to

3. Match.

1. You've never been to Peru, 2 a. isn't it?
2. It's interesting, 2 b. is it?
3. You worked in a bank, 3 c. can you?
4. You didn't work at the bank very long, 4 d. have you?
5. The book isn't that great, 5 e. did you?
6. You can't work late tonight, 6 f. didn't you?

2. How was it?

1 ► Eric is describing his summer vacation to a friend. Listen to the conversation and look at the pictures. Circle *G* for *good* or *B* for *bad* to describe his opinions.

G B
1. flight

G B
2. scenery

G B
3. hotel

G B
4. food

2 ► Listen to the three possible conversations and practice them with a partner.
► Have similar conversations, using the questions in the box and your own ideas.

A Did you do anything special over the summer?

B I took a trip to Mexico.
A Oh, really? How was it?
B Wonderful! It was one of the nicest vacations I've ever taken.

B I took a trip to Mexico.
A Oh, really? How was it?
B Not that great.

B No, not really. How about you? . . .

Did you . . .

do anything special read any good books see any good movies go anywhere interesting	over	the summer? the weekend? the holiday? vacation?

Other ways to say it

What did you think of it?
How did you like it?
Did you enjoy it?
Did you have a good time?
Was it any good?

Acapulco, Mexico

3 ► Study the frame: The superlative of adjectives with the present perfect

It's	one of	the nicest places	I've ever	been to.
		the most boring books		read.
	the worst/best movie			seen.
	the least/most useful course			taken.

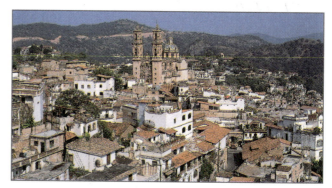

Taxco, Mexico

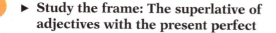 boring - скучный

least (i.) - наименьший, меньший

4
- ▶ Complete the movie review. Use the superlatives of the adjectives in parentheses.
- ▶ Listen to check your work.

Movie Watch

First the bad news: The new lineup of summer movies is probably _the worst_ (bad) we've had in years, starting with *The Return of the Dragon Slayers*. Give us a break! This is one of _the silliest_ (silly) and _the most_ (violent) films of the year. Then there's *Cowboy Boots*, _the most_ (boring) western I've ever seen. I actually fell asleep during _the most_ (exciting) scene! Can you believe that? And you can skip *Falling Out of Love*. It must be _dumbest_ (dumb) and _the most_ (childish) romantic comedy that director Andy Lewis has ever made. However, there's *some* good news: It's *Over the Top*, one of _the most_ (original) films I've seen this season, and quite possibly _the best_ (good) movie of the year. Incredibly, this is one of _the most_ _least_ (expensive) commercial films ever made. The movie was produced by a group of university film students on a shoestring budget. Hollywood can learn a lesson from these young filmmakers!

5 ▶ Answer each of the following questions, using the superlative form of an adjective with the present perfect. You may choose one of the adjectives in parentheses or think of your own.

1. How is that English course you're taking? (useful, easy, difficult)
   It's one of the easiest courses I've ever taken.
2. I see you're reading *War and Peace*. Do you like it? (exciting, boring, good)
3. What did you think of the film festival? (fascinating, enjoyable, disappointing)
4. I heard you stayed at the Park Hotel. How did you like it? (modern, expensive, clean)
5. I've never eaten at the Hard Rock. Is it any good? (unusual, bad, reasonable)
6. I hear you've met Ed's sister. What's she like? (friendly, nice, shy)

6 ▶ Work with a partner. Ask and answer questions about your favorite and least favorite things, using the pictures below.

A *What's the best movie you've ever seen?*
B Gone with the Wind. *I've seen it eight times.*
A *Really? What's the worst movie you've ever seen?*
B The Night of the Living Dead. *I thought it was disgusting!*

movie

book

vacation

meal

▶ Act out similar conversations, using your own ideas. Keep the conversations going by asking additional questions.

3. What's new?

1 ► Listen to the conversation.

► Act out similar conversations with a partner, using the sentences in the box.

A What's new?
B I'm not working at the camera store anymore.
A You aren't? Where are you working now?
B At a bank.
A You are? I didn't know that.

> I'm not . . .
>
> working at the post office anymore. (at the telephone company)
> working at night anymore. (during the day)
> driving to work anymore. (by bus)
> living with my family anymore. (in my own apartment)

2 ► Study the frame: Rejoinders showing interest or surprise

I'm an opera singer.	**You are**?
School's closing early today.	**It is**?
Sue isn't going to school this term.	**She's not?/She isn't**?
I don't like ice cream.	**You don't**?
My parents took a trip to Peru.	**They did**?
Rick used to be a rock star.	**He did**?
I didn't take a vacation last year.	**You didn't**?
I can lend you some money.	**You can**?
I can't ride a bicycle.	**You can't**?
We won't have time to go today.	**We won't**?
Meg has worked here for twenty years.	**She has**?
Jan hasn't started her term paper yet.	**She hasn't**?

3 ► Match the statements with the reactions.

1. I'm not working at the bank anymore. b
2. My sister just had a baby. a
3. My parents don't live in Montreal anymore. e
4. I've decided to go back to school. c
5. My brother is going to get married. d

a. She did?
b. You aren't?/You're not?
c. You have?
d. He is?
e. They don't?

4 ► Work with a partner. React with surprise to the following statements, using rejoinders.

1. My uncle speaks twelve languages fluently. *He does?*
2. The Kasugas just won a trip for two around the world.
3. I've never had a hamburger.
4. English isn't her native language.
5. I'll take you out to dinner tonight.
6. I used to live in Australia.

5 ► Listen to the statements and react with surprise, using rejoinders like the ones in exercise 2.

► Now think of two surprising statements of your own and get your partner's reaction.

4. It's exciting, isn't it?

1 ▶ **Study the frames: Tag questions**

Affirmative statement + negative tag			Negative statement + affirmative tag		
The book is exciting,	**isn't it?**	↘	The book isn't very exciting,	**is it?**	↘
It looks interesting,	**doesn't it?**	↘	It doesn't look very interesting,	**does it?**	↘
Tom Clancy wrote it,	**didn't he?**	↗	Tom Clancy didn't write it,	**did he?**	↗
He's written other books,	**hasn't he?**	↗	He hasn't written anything recently,	**has he?**	↗

> You usually say tag questions with rising intonation (↗) when you are asking questions and want information. You usually say tag questions with falling intonation (↘) when you are giving your opinion and want to know if the other person agrees.

2 ▶ **Listen to the four possible conversations and practice them with a partner.**

 A Soccer is a really exciting game, isn't it?

B Yes, it really is.   **B** To tell you the truth, I don't think it's *that* exciting.

 A Soccer isn't a very exciting game, is it?

B No, it really isn't.   **B** Actually, I think it's *very* exciting.

> It's not *that* exciting. = It's not as exciting as you think.

▶ **Act out similar conversations, using the information under the pictures below.**
▶ **Have similar conversations with your partner about topics that are interesting to you.**

Some people think soccer is a very exciting game. Others think it's boring.

Some people think fast food is really good. Others think it's awful.

Some people think royal families are very interesting. Others don't think they're interesting at all.

Some people thought Greta Garbo was the most fascinating woman in the world.

3 ▶ **Complete the following sentences by adding a tag question to each one.**
▶ **Find out how well you know another student by asking the questions below, changing the words in italics when necessary.**

1. Your name is *Yoshi*, <u>isn't it</u> ?
2. You're from *Tokyo*, ___ ?
3. You've lived here *for three years*, ___ ?
4. You work *in a hospital*, ___ ?
5. You've never been to *New Zealand*, ___ ?
6. You weren't in my *English* class last semester, ___ ?

5. I was wondering . . .

Anita Rivera is talking to her husband, Ed, who has just come home from work. The Riveras moved into a new apartment over the weekend.

1

Anita You know, I think taking exams and writing papers is going to seem like a vacation after moving.

Ed Yeah, it was a relief to go to work today.

Anita So, what's new at the office?

Ed Nothing much. It was a pretty routine day. Anything interesting happen to you?

Anita Well, I ran into Carol Thomas.

Ed Oh, you did? How is she?

Anita Fine. She seemed pretty surprised when I told her I was starting graduate school. She thought I was still working at the bank.

Ed Did you give her our new address?

Anita No, I didn't get a chance. She was in a hurry.

Ed You know, we should invite Carol and John over. We haven't gotten together with them in a long time.

Anita Sure, as soon as we've finished unpacking.

Ed Say, I was wondering if you'd like to take a break and go out to eat? I mean, I'd like to cook you a candlelight dinner, but I don't know how long it would take to find any pots and pans in all these boxes!

Anita Sounds good to me. Let's go!
(Phone rings)

2. Figure it out

Say *True, False,* or *It doesn't say.*

1. Ed works in an office.   *True*
2. Ed had an exciting day at work.
3. Anita is a graduate student.
4. Anita still works at a bank.
5. The Riveras moved because they needed a larger apartment.
6. Anita invited Carol and John to dinner.
7. Ed and Anita haven't finished unpacking.
8. Ed is going to cook dinner after he finds some pots and pans.

3. Listen in

Anita is talking to her mother on the phone. Read the questions below. Then listen to two parts of the conversation and choose *a* or *b* when you hear the question, "What did Anita's mother just say?"

1. What did Anita's mother just say?
   a. Fine. In fact, I'm coming to Berkeley next weekend.
   b. Fine. In fact, I'll be in Berkeley next weekend.

2. What did Anita's mother just say?
   a. Mrs. Davis is driving. You remember her, don't you?
   b. Mrs. Davis is driving. It's all right if I visit, isn't it?

6. Your turn

Work in groups. Complete the following sentences with answers from the box. The answers to this exercise are on page 165.

1. The highest waterfall in the world is in _Venezuela_ .
2. The longest wall in the world is in _China St!_
3. The longest street in the world is in _Yonge St!_
4. The most popular country for tourists is _Venfrance_
5. The longest rivers in the world are _Mississippi Nile Amazon_ and _the Amazon_
6. The largest ocean in the world is _the Pacific_
7. The place with the densest automobile traffic in the world is _New York_
8. The city with the largest taxi fleet is _Mexico_
9. The coldest place in the world is in _Antarctica_
10. The longest mountain range in the world is _Himalayas Andes_

Mexico City	Tokyo	the Amazon
the Atlantic	the United States	Italy
New York City	the Nile	the Himalayas
the Pacific	Canada	China
Hong Kong	the Mississippi	the Andes
France	Venezuela	Antarctica

Answer these questions about your country. Discuss your answers in groups.

1. What is the highest mountain?
2. What is the oldest city?
3. What is the hottest area? The coldest area?
4. What is the most popular tourist spot?

Now answer these questions about yourself. Compare your answers with classmates.

1. What's the hottest place you've ever been? The coldest?
2. What's the most interesting city, country, or place you've ever visited?
3. Who is the most famous person you've ever met or seen in person?
4. What was the best day you've ever had?

How to say it

Practice the conversation.

A Guess what? I just got a new job.

B You did? Congratulations.

A But I have to work on Saturdays.

B You do? That's not so good.

The highest waterfall in the world is Angel Falls in Venezuela. It is 3,212 feet (979 meters) high.

This is the longest wall in the world. The main part of the wall is over 2,000 miles (1250 kilometers) long.

The longest street in the world is Yonge Street. Its official length is over 1,100 miles (687 kilometers).

7. MACHU PICCHU:
GHOST CITY IN THE CLOUDS

The city of Machu Picchu is one of the great mysteries of the world. It is an ancient city on a mountain high in the Peruvian Andes. A beautiful and mysterious site, it is completely isolated.

Look at the picture of Machu Picchu and the title of the article. What do you think the article is about? Write some questions about Machu Picchu and then see if they are answered in the article.

In 1911, Yale University professor Hiram Bingham "discovered" Machu Picchu during an expedition in the Andes. Actually, local people led him to the site of the ruins, covered with jungle growth. Bingham believed that these ruins were the last capital of the Inca empire, "the lost city of the Incas."

Was Bingham right? There's been much discussion by archeologists in the absence of any written record of Machu Picchu. It is generally agreed that the city was built during the fifteenth century and abandoned in the sixteenth century at the time of the Spanish conquest. It may have been built as a fortress to protect the Incas from the conquering Spaniards or from neighboring tribes who attacked Machu Picchu. It may have been a holy city where religious rites were performed, perhaps by chosen women. (About three-quarters of the skeletons found at Machu Picchu are female.)

The ruins of Machu Picchu consist of agricultural, residential, and sacred zones in an area of about two square miles. Approximately 1,000 people lived there once. Over 200 stone buildings were used as homes, temples, and warehouses for the corn and potatoes that were the main foods for the Incas. To grow these crops, along with other plants, the Incas designed a system of terraces and steps alongside the mountain to prevent erosion. They also built stone aqueducts and irrigation canals to provide water for the crops. The Incas even invented the first dehydrated food, called *chuño,* a type of dried potato.

The sacred buildings of Machu Picchu show the extraordinary skill of the Incas in architectural design and stonework. The Temple of the Sun, perhaps the most beautiful structure, is one of the highest points in the city. Some say it may once have been covered with gems. Yet despite the Incas' advanced knowledge of engineering and expert stonework, they didn't have a written language. That is perhaps the greatest barrier to uncovering the mysteries of the ghost city in the clouds.

1. Say *True* or *False*.

1. The Inca ruins at Machu Picchu are about 500 years old.
2. The Incas left behind a written history of Machu Picchu.
3. The Incas who built Machu Picchu were skilled in architecture and stonework.
4. Archeologists are now sure that Machu Picchu was a holy city.
5. We still don't know everything about Machu Picchu.

2. Why do you think the author calls Machu Picchu "the ghost city in the clouds"? Give as many possible reasons as you can.

No one has lived there for more than 400 years.

3. What mysterious cities, ruins, or other structures do you know of? Can you think of any explanation or theory for their existence?

PREVIEW

FUNCTIONS/THEMES	LANGUAGE	FORMS
Talk about likes and dislikes	How do you like living here? I love it. I miss being near my family.	
State a preference	Would you like to study for the test now, or would you rather take it easy? I'd just as soon take it easy. It doesn't matter to me.	
Talk about habits	I'm not used to getting up early.	*Be used to*
Complain	I'm so tired. It's such a long trip. I'm not used to so much work.	*So* vs. *such*
Express anticipation Talk about strengths and weaknesses	I'm looking forward to going to the play tonight. You must be good at learning languages. I have a hard time learning languages.	Gerunds

Preview the conversations.

You speak English so well. You sound almost like a native.

Well, you seem to get along really well. You must be good at languages.

Not quite. I still make a lot of mistakes.

Read the conversation above. Work with a partner and act out a similar conversation about your progress in English. Use the sentences below or your own ideas.

1. I still make a lot of mistakes. / I used to make a lot of mistakes.
2. My vocabulary is still limited. / My vocabulary is growing.
3. I still have trouble expressing myself. / I used to have trouble expressing myself.
4. I have trouble with pronunciation. / I used to have trouble with pronunciation.
5. I had a hard time understanding people at first. / I can understand a lot more than I used to.

UNIT 2 • LESSONS 8 — 14

8. How do you like living in Taiwan?

David is visiting his cousin Mary, who has been working at an import-export company in Taipei, Taiwan, for two years.

A

David I'm impressed. When you gave directions to the taxi driver, you sounded just like a native.

Mary Well, not quite. I still have trouble expressing myself.

David Didn't you already speak some Chinese when you got here?

Mary A little. But I used to make so many mistakes, and I had a lot of trouble with the pronunciation. I also had a hard time understanding people, especially when they spoke fast.

David Do you understand everything now?

Mary Not everything. My vocabulary is still limited.

David Well, you seem to get along really well. You must be good at languages. I've always found them difficult.

B

David So, how do you like living in Taiwan?

Mary I love it. Taipei is such a fascinating city. Of course, I get homesick at times. I miss seeing my family and friends.

David Did you have any trouble getting used to the way of life here?

Mary Oh, sure, a little at first. But I'm pretty used to it by now.

David Gee, look at all those motorcycles! . . . I'm going to have trouble getting across the street!

Mary Don't worry. You'll get used to the traffic. Everyone does.

David I hope so. I'm looking forward to seeing Taipei. I hear the Chinese temples are really worth seeing, too.

Mary Yes, you should definitely see some of them. Would you like to go sightseeing this afternoon, or would you rather wait until tomorrow?

David I'd just as soon get some sleep this afternoon. I'm so tired after such a long trip. I guess I'm not used to so much traveling.

Mary Yes, and there's the time difference too. It takes a few days.

Figure it out

1. Listen to the conversations and choose *a* or *b*.

1. a. Mary speaks Chinese perfectly.
   b. Mary speaks Chinese fairly well.

2. a. Mary learned to speak Chinese fluently before she went to Taiwan.
   b. Mary learned Chinese mostly after she got to Taiwan.

3. a. David has a hard time learning languages.
   b. David wants to learn Chinese.

4. a. Mary enjoys living in Taiwan.
   b. Mary wants to return home because she's homesick.

5. a. David thinks the traffic in Taiwan is heavy.
   b. David is already used to the traffic in Taiwan.

6. a. This is David's first visit to Taipei.
   b. David has been to Taipei before.

7. a. David would like to visit some Chinese temples this afternoon.
   b. David wants to rest this afternoon.

2. Find another way to say it.

1. not really
2. It was difficult for me to understand people.
3. I've grown accustomed to it.
4. Most people get used to it.
5. I'd prefer to sleep.

3. Complete each sentence with *so* or *such*.

1. I'm _so_ tired.
2. It's _____ an exciting city.
3. It's _____ a difficult language.
4. I'm not used to _____ much traveling.
5. It's _____ fascinating.

9. I'm not used to getting up early.

1
- ▶ Listen to Celia talk about living in Toronto and take notes.
- ▶ What does Celia say about the things in the box? Listen again and write your answers under the headings *Likes* and *Dislikes*.

> the people in Toronto
> friends and family back home
> the restaurants, shops,
>   and neighborhoods
>
> Brazilian food
> the streets and
>   subways
> English

Likes

- *She likes the people in Toronto.* _____
- _____
- _____

Dislikes

- *She misses her friends and family back home.*
- _____
- _____

2
- ▶ Listen to the conversation and practice it with a partner.
- ▶ Act out similar conversations, using the information in the boxes and the pictures below.

A I've lived in this city for three years.
B How do you like living here?
A I like it a lot, but I miss being near my family.

> **How do you like . . .**
>
> living here?
> working there?
> studying Spanish?
> being married?
> living so far from home?

> **Some responses**
>
> I like it a lot.
> I love it.
> I enjoy exploring the city.
> I find it difficult at times.
> I miss being near my family.
> I get homesick at times.
> I miss my old job.
> I miss my independence at times.

I've lived in this city for three years.

I've worked at Smith Brothers since the summer.

I'm studying Spanish.

I've been married for a year.

3
- ▶ Work with a partner. Act out conversations similar to the ones in exercise 2. Use the topics in the box or your own ideas.

> **Some topics**
>
> A hobby
> Someone you work with
> Your home or neighborhood
>
> A course you're taking
> A sport you play
> A musical instrument you play

4
- ▶ Listen to the two possible conversations and practice them with a partner.
- ▶ Act out similar conversations.

A Would you like to study for the test now, or would you rather take it easy?

> **Some alternatives**
>
> study for the test now or take it easy
> eat a big meal or have something light
> do something outdoors or stay indoors
> go out tonight or not do anything special

> **Other ways to say it**
>
> I'd rather stay home.
> I'd rather not go out.

B I'd just as soon take it easy.   **B** It doesn't matter to me.

5 ▶ Dave and Frank are spending the weekend at a health spa. Listen to their conversation and check (√) the things Dave usually does on weekends.

☐ gets up at 6:00 A.M.
☐ exercises before breakfast
☐ has a big breakfast
☐ walks the dog
☐ goes running
☐ watches TV

6 ▶ Listen to the two possible conversations and practice them with a partner.
▶ Act out similar conversations, using the pictures and phrases below and the information in the box.

A Let's turn on the radio. Is that O.K. with you?

B Sure. I'm used to studying with music.

B Actually, I'd rather not. I'm not used to studying with music.

I'm (not) used to . . .

studying with music.
walking long distances.
singing in front of people.
staying up late.
taking long vacations.
getting up early.

turn on the radio

meet for breakfast at 6:30 A.M.

go for a 10-mile hike

go to the midnight show

take a 4-week vacation

sing at the class party

7 ▶ Work with a partner. Suggest something you'd like to do. Your partner will accept or refuse. Use the conversations in exercise 6 as a model.

10. I'm so tired!

1 ▶ Listen to people complaining. Match each conversation with the picture it describes.

2 ▶ Listen to the conversation and practice it with a partner.
▶ Act out similar conversations, using the information in the boxes.

A I'm so tired!
B How come?
A (I guess) I'm not used to getting up so early.

Some complaints

I'm so tired!
I've got such a headache!
I've got such a stomachache!

Some reasons

I'm not used to . . .
  getting up so early.
  speaking so much English.
  eating such spicy food.
  studying so hard.
  such long hours.
  so much homework.

3 ▶ Study the frames: *So* vs. *such*

So + adjective or adverb	*So* + *much* or *many*	*Such* + adjective + noun
I'm **so tired**. You speak English **so well**.	I'm not used to **so much** food. I'm not used to **so many** people.	It's **such a long trip**. They're **such nice people**.

4 ▶ Complete the letter with *so* or *such*.

Dear Gloria,
Thanks for writing me _such_ a long letter. I don't have time to write _such_ long letters these days because I have _so_ much work. I've been working sixty hours a week lately! I know I shouldn't work _so_ hard. There are _so_ many other important things in life, but you know how it is.
We haven't seen each other in _such_ a long time. I've thought of going to see you, but it's _so_ expensive to fly. As you know, I'm not used to driving _such_ long distances, but maybe I will soon. Anyway, I'll talk to you in a few weeks.
Love,
Victor

5 ▶ Complain to your partner about something that's bothering you, using *so* or *such*. Then explain the reason.

11. You must be good at learning languages.

1 ▶ What are these people looking forward to doing?
Match the sentences in the box with the pictures.
▶ Listen to check your work.

I'm looking forward to . . .

a. seeing my family over
   the holiday.
b. sleeping late tomorrow.
c. going to the play tonight.
d. starting my new class
   next week.

1. _____

2. _____

3. _____

4. _____

2 ▶ Listen to the conversation and practice it with a partner.
▶ Talk about things you're good at or not so good at. Use the
phrases in the box or your own information.

Are you good at . . .

learning languages?
remembering names?
speaking in front of groups?
making small talk?
singing in tune?

A You speak English almost perfectly. You must
be good at learning languages.
B I guess I'm lucky. I've always found it easy.
A Not me. I have trouble learning languages.

Other ways to say it

I have a hard time learning
languages.

3 ▶ Study the frames: Gerunds

Verb + gerund	Preposition + gerund	Other expressions + gerund
I **enjoy traveling**. I **miss seeing** my old friends. I **dislike taking** long flights.	I'm used **to living** far from home. I'm good **at fixing** cars. I'm thinking **of moving** to Taiwan. I'm looking forward **to seeing** some Chinese temples.	I **have trouble speaking** Chinese. I **have a hard time understanding** people. Taipei **is worth seeing**.

All of these verbs and expressions can also be followed by nouns. *Have trouble*
and *have a hard time* take the preposition *with* before a noun.
   I have trouble *with* languages.   I have a hard time *with* pronunciation.

4 ▶ Answer these questions, using a gerund in each answer.
▶ Compare your answers with your classmates' answers.

1. What is something you're looking forward to?
2. What is something you're thinking of doing
   this weekend?
3. What do you miss when you travel?
4. What is something in your country that
   tourists should see? (*is worth*)

5. What is something you enjoy?
6. What is something you're good at?
7. What is something you dislike doing?
8. What is something you have trouble doing?
9. What is something you're not used to doing?

12. I'm going to miss having him around.

Lou Miller is having lunch with his friend John Thomas.

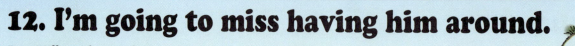

1

John So, you lost your assistant?

Lou Yeah, Bill decided to move back to Vancouver just last week. Now I have to find someone else.

John Well, it shouldn't be hard to find someone to take his place, should it? This town must be full of cabinetmakers.

Lou Maybe, but not many who are as good as Bill. I'm going to miss having him around.

John Well, maybe it's worth looking around before you hire just anyone.

Lou Hey, you wouldn't happen to know a good cabinetmaker who's out of work, would you?

John I wish I did, Lou. I'll keep my ears open, though. Maybe I'll hear of someone . . . . Look, I'd better get back to work.

Lou O.K., thanks, John. Take it easy.

(A young woman sitting nearby comes up to Lou.)

Kate Excuse me . . . I couldn't help overhearing your conversation. I happen to be a cabinetmaker, and I can start work right away.

2. Figure it out

Say *True*, *False*, or *It doesn't say*.

1. Bill used to work for Lou.
2. Bill lived in Vancouver before.
3. Lou doesn't think Bill is a good cabinetmaker.
4. John used to be a cabinetmaker.
5. Lou knows who he wants to hire.
6. John knows a lot of cabinetmakers who can take Bill's place.
7. If John hears of anyone who can work with Lou, he'll let him know.

3. Listen in

Kate and Lou continue their conversation. Read the statements below. Then listen to the conversation and say *True* or *False*.

1. Kate just learned how to make cabinets.
2. Kate is going to have an interview with Lou tomorrow morning.

13. Your turn

Mr. Zolis runs an English-language school on Tolo, an island in the Pacific Ocean. He is looking for a new director. All of the following people have applied for the position, and he has to decide which of them will be best for it. Read the description of Tolo and the information about each candidate. Work in groups to decide who you think Mr. Zolis should hire for the job.

- Tolo is a very isolated island. There is no television or radio.
- There are few foreigners, and not many Toloese speak a foreign language well.
- The Toloese usually accept foreigners who speak Toloese and try to follow their customs.
- Most married women with children do not work, although this is slowly changing.
- Most of the students and teachers at the language school are male.
- There is only one public school on Tolo for children between the ages of 6 and 18.
- The Toloese have great respect for older people. Mr. Zolis is 62 years old.

CANDIDATES

	DAVE	MARIAN	PAUL	CAROL
AGE	28	33	37	50
MARITAL STATUS	single	divorced	married	married, but husband cannot come with her
DEPENDENTS	none	2-year-old son	three children (8, 12, and 15 years old)	none
OVERSEAS EXPERIENCE	lived in Paris for 1 year during college	worked abroad for 7 years; lived in Tolo for 6 months	has traveled in Europe and South America	lived on another island for 2 years
TEACHING EXPERIENCE	5 years	7 years	12 years	20 years
PERSONALITY	very enthusiastic	flexible; likes island life	confident and easygoing	very competent, but difficult to please
LANGUAGES	speaks fluent French	speaks Toloese fairly well	speaks fluent German	speaks another language similar to Toloese

▶ Which of these people would you hire for a similar position in your country? Discuss the reasons for your choice in groups.

How to say it

Practice the conversation.

A You look so happy! How come?

B Because I'm having such a good time!

14.

OUTLOOK:
LIVING ABROAD

Jane Baxter, an American teacher, has just returned to the United States after living in Japan for five years. In this interview, she talks about her experience living abroad.

"Living in another culture is like seeing the world through a new pair of glasses."

Before you read the article, look at the quotation above. What happens when you put on a new pair of glasses? How can this experience be similar to living in a foreign country?

INTERVIEWER Jane, you've recently returned from Japan. How long did you live there?

JANE For five years.

INTERVIEWER And why did you go to Japan in the first place?

JANE Well, a Japanese exchange student was living with my family, and he got me interested in going to Japan. He encouraged me try to get a teaching job there and even offered me a place to stay until I found an apartment—at his mother's house in Tokyo.

INTERVIEWER So you went?

JANE I did. When I arrived his mother was very helpful, but she didn't speak much English and I didn't speak any Japanese. We managed to communicate, somehow, with gestures and mime, or sometimes we would both use dictionaries.

INTERVIEWER In what ways is life in Japan different from life in the United States?

JANE In just about every aspect. A big change was using public transportation in Tokyo instead of a car. Trains, subways, and other transportation in Japan is very good, though crowded. You get used to shopping more often, because, without a car, you have to carry your groceries home. But I was really glad to be rid of my car. Another thing is the low crime rate in Tokyo and other big cities in Japan. I always felt safe and never worried about crime. That's pretty unusual in almost any big city in the world today.

INTERVIEWER Did you have any difficulties adjusting?

JANE Well, at the beginning it was hard not knowing the language. At first I learned survival Japanese, so I could get by in everyday situations, but anything technical was difficult for me to understand. I took classes, but it was slow going, and I didn't always express myself because I was afraid of making mistakes. I wish I had taken more risks—I would probably have learned the language faster. Another thing I had to get used to was living in a culture where the majority of people looked different from me. I knew I'd always be an outsider in some ways.

INTERVIEWER What about Japanese food?

JANE Overall, the diet there is a healthy one— low fat. Oh, there were many Japanese specialties that I liked, and others that I didn't like so much. The food was very different, but I didn't expect to eat American style there. I expected to eat Japanese style and to buy Japanese products. I think Japanese food preparation takes a long time though, and I didn't have a lot of time to prepare food, so much of my experience comes from eating in restaurants.

INTERVIEWER What advice would you give to someone going to live overseas for the first time?

JANE Do some of the things I *didn't* do: Before you go, read as much as you can. Find out about the culture, the customs, the holidays, the traditions. Learn a little bit of the language if you can . . . and the way people express politeness. Be flexible. Living in another culture is like seeing the world through a new pair of glasses— at first everything looks confusing. But if you keep your eyes open, eventually everything becomes clear. Unfortunately, a lot of people just close their eyes.

Read the article. Then imagine you are having a conversation with Jane. Which of these statements do you think she would make? Check (√) the ones you think she would say.

1. I knew my Japanese was bad, but I took every opportunity to try to speak the language.
2. I missed having a car in Japan.
3. I ate Japanese food frequently while I was there.
4. It was frustrating at first because I could only express myself in simple, basic ways.
5. I wish I had learned more about the country and culture before I went.

PREVIEW

FUNCTIONS/THEMES	LANGUAGE	FORMS
Ask about and confirm facts	Who's it by? It was written by Shakespeare. Dostoyevsky wrote *War and Peace*, didn't he? No, *War and Peace* was written by Tolstoy.	The passive in the past tense
Talk about famous landmarks and famous works	The Pyramids at Giza were built around 2500 B.C.	The passive without an agent
React to news	My wife was just promoted to manager. That's really good news. My husband was laid off a couple of weeks ago. I'm sorry to hear that.	
Talk about needs Ask a friend for information	I need someone to take care of my daughter. What kind of person are you looking for? Someone who's good with children. Do you know of anyone who baby-sits and can cook? I have a friend whose son likes to baby-sit.	Relative clauses with *who* and *whose*
Talk about the content of something	What's it about? It's about a group of Chinese women who live in San Francisco.	

Preview the conversations.

Who's taking care of the children?

More women in the United States are working outside the home than ever before. Nowadays, only a small minority of families with children follow the traditional pattern of working fathers and stay-at-home mothers.

Because women have traditionally taken care of children, we might ask who is taking care of them now, with so many mothers and fathers both at work. Sometimes children are minded by the working parents themselves: when they work at home, in their own businesses, or even at the office. However, the most common arrangement is for children to be watched by baby-sitting relatives, such as grandparents. Another option, taken by about one-fourth of working parents, is "family day-care providers," who look after children in their own homes. Another one-fourth of the children are placed in day-care centers, normally staffed by licensed care-givers. A smaller number are cared for at home by paid baby-sitters (sometimes called "nannies"), which is

by far the most expensive choice. Then there are the "latchkey kids," school-aged children who go home after school to empty houses with no one to take care of them.

Read the article. Then work with a partner and discuss these questions.

1. In your country, do married women with children work outside the home? If so, who takes care of their children?
2. Which of the child-care arrangements discussed in the article do you think is the best?
3. What kind of person would you want to take care of your children? (*Someone who . . .*)

Unit 3 **21**

15. What kind of person are you looking for?

When Jane arrives at work, she finds Barbara reading the classified ads.

A

Jane Good morning!

Barbara Oh, good morning, Jane.

Jane What are you reading the classifieds for?

Barbara I need someone to take care of my little girl after school.

Jane What kind of person are you looking for?

Barbara Oh, you know, someone who's mature . . . someone who's good with children . . . a responsible person I can count on who's willing to make dinner once in a while if I have to work late. Why? Do you know of anyone?

Jane Well, I have a friend whose son likes to baby-sit. He seems very mature. I'm not sure if he can cook, though.

Barbara Well, it's worth a try.

Jane I'll write down his number for you. At least that's one problem I don't have.

Barbara Why do you say that?

Jane My husband stays home with the kids now. He was laid off a couple of weeks ago.

Barbara Oh, Jane, I didn't know. I'm sorry to hear that.

Figure it out

1. Listen to the conversations and say *True, False,* or *It doesn't say.*

1. Barbara has only one child.
2. Barbara works late from time to time.
3. Barbara's husband doesn't know how to cook.
4. Barbara isn't interested in calling the friend's son.
5. Jane's husband recently lost his job.
6. Barbara doesn't like *The Joy Luck Club*.

2. Find another way to say it.

1. someone I can depend on
2. What do you mean?
3. someone to look after my daughter
4. What's the subject?
5. He lost his job.

3. Do the sentences in each pair have the same meaning or different meanings? Say *Same* or *Different.*

1. What are you reading the classifieds for?
   Why are you reading the classifieds?   *Same*

2. He seems very mature.
   He seems very young.

3. Who wrote it?
   Who's it by?

4. But I'm not sure if he can cook.
   I'm not sure if he can cook, though.

5. I'm looking for someone who can count.
   I'm looking for someone I can count on.

6. *The Woman Warrior* was written by Maxine Hong Kingston.
   Maxine Hong Kingston wrote *The Woman Warrior*.

B

Jane Aren't you going to have lunch, Barbara?

Barbara No, I'm not hungry. Besides, I'd rather read my book.

Jane *The Joy Luck Club* . . . What's it about?

Barbara Well, it's about a group of Chinese women who live in San Francisco. The main character is an American-born woman whose mother came from China.

Jane It sounds interesting. Who's it by?

Barbara Amy Tan.

Jane She wrote *The Woman Warrior*, too, didn't she?

Barbara No, that was written by Maxine Hong Kingston.

16. Who's it by?

1 ▶ Listen and match each conversation with the picture it describes.

2 ▶ Listen to the two possible conversations and practice them with a partner.
▶ Act out similar conversations, using the incorrect information in the box and your own knowledge.

A Dostoyevsky wrote *War and Peace*, didn't he?

B No, *War and Peace* was written by Tolstoy.

B I'm not sure who wrote it.

Some incorrect information

War and Peace was written by Dostoyevsky.
The telephone was invented by Edison.
The *Mona Lisa* was painted by Michelangelo.
Madame Butterfly was composed by Mozart.
The phonograph was invented by Bell.

3 ▶ Study the frames: The passive in the past tense

The active in the past tense			The passive in the past tense			
Subject (agent)	Past tense verb	Object	Subject	Past of *be*	Past participle	*by* + agent
Tolstoy	wrote	*War and Peace.*	*War and Peace*	**was**	**written**	**by Tolstoy**.
Edison	invented	the electric light bulb and the phonograph.	The electric light bulb and the phonograph	**were**	**invented**	**by Edison**.

TALK ABOUT FAMOUS LANDMARKS AND FAMOUS WORKS • THE PASSIVE WITHOUT AN AGENT

4 ▶ **Study the frame: The passive without an agent**

Subject	Past of *be*	Past participle	
The Pyramids at Giza	were	built	around 2500 B.C.
My son	was	fired	last week.

When it is unnecessary to name the agent or if the agent is unknown, it is omitted in passive sentences.
The Pyramids at Giza were built around 2500 B.C. =
  Someone built the Pyramids at Giza around 2500 B.C.
My son was fired last week = "They" fired my son
  last week.

5 ▶ **Work with a partner. Look at the pictures and discuss what you know about them.**
▶ **Make up sentences about these famous places and works, using the passive without an agent.**

The Pyramids at Giza, Egypt
Built: around 2500 B.C.
The Pyramids at Giza were built around 2500 B.C.

Stonehenge in England
Constructed: more than 4,000 years ago

Cave paintings at Altamira, Spain
Painted: between 15,000 B.C. and 10,000 B.C.

The city of Machu Picchu in Peru
Built: over 450 years ago

6 ▶ **Talk about other famous places or works. Do you know when they were made / built / painted / composed / written?**

REACT TO NEWS

7 ▶ **Listen to the two possible conversations and practice them with a partner.**
▶ **Act out similar conversations, using the news in the box or your own news.**

A Did I tell you?

A My wife was just promoted to manager.
B I'm glad to hear that. That's really good news.

A My husband was laid off a couple of weeks ago.
B I'm sorry to hear that. That's really too bad.

Some news

My wife was just promoted to manager.
My husband was laid off a couple of weeks ago.
My son was just accepted into Harvard.
My daughter was fired yesterday.
My parents were evicted from their apartment last week.
I was just hired by Super Software Systems.

17. I'm looking for someone . . .

1 ▶ **A man is calling an employment agency. Listen to the telephone conversation and check (√) the requirements for the job he is calling about.**

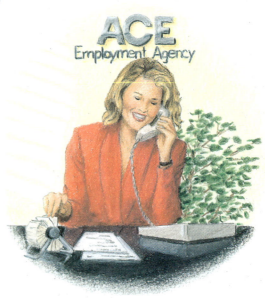

ACE Employment Agency

2 ▶ **Listen to the conversation and practice it with a partner.**
▶ **Imagine you are looking for someone to do some work. Act out similar conversations, using the information in the boxes or your own ideas.**

A I need someone to take care of my daughter.
B What kind of person are you looking for?
A Someone who's good with children.

I need someone to . . .

take care of my daughter.
help me out in the office.
build some cabinets.

I'm looking for someone . . .

who's good with children.
who's experienced.
who's willing to make dinner
 if I have to work late.

who's mature.
who I can trust.
who can type well.
who I can count on.

3 ▶ **Study the frame: Relative clauses with *who* and *whose***

I have a friend. I have a friend	She **who**	needs a job.
I know someone. I know someone	He's **who's**	good with children.
I have a friend. I have a friend	Her **whose**	son likes to baby-sit.
I know a couple. I know a couple	Their **whose**	daughter is looking for part-time work.

Whose and *who's* have the same pronunciation.

4 ▶ **Listen to the two possible conversations and practice them with the same partner as in exercise 2.**
▶ **Ask if your partner knows anyone who can help you. Use the information in the boxes or your own ideas.**

A Do you know of anyone who baby-sits and can cook?

B I have a friend whose son likes to baby-sit. I'm not sure if he can cook, though.

B Not offhand.

Do you know of anyone . . .

who baby-sits and can cook?
who's looking for a secretarial job?
who knows how to build cabinets?

I have a friend . . .

whose son likes to baby-sit.
whose daughter is a terrific typist.
whose wife is an experienced cabinetmaker.

18. What's it about?

1
- ▶ **Listen to the conversation and practice it with a partner.**
- ▶ **Say what each novel is about by combining the sentences. Use relative clauses with *who* or *whose*.**
- ▶ **Act out similar conversations with your partner.**

A What are you reading?
B *The Joy Luck Club.*
A What's it about?
B It's about a group of Chinese women who live in San Francisco. The main character is an American-born woman whose mother came from China.
A Who's it by?
B Amy Tan.

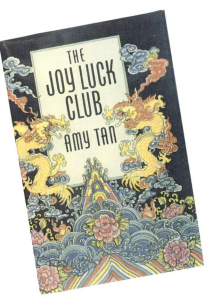

The Joy Luck Club, by Amy Tan, is about a group of Chinese women. The women live in San Francisco. The main character is an American-born woman. The woman's mother came from China.

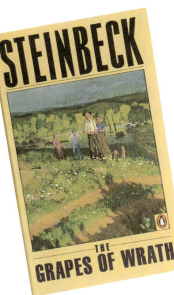

The Grapes of Wrath, by John Steinbeck, is about a family. They travel to California during the Great Depression of the 1930s in search of a better life.

The Handmaid's Tale, by Margaret Atwood, is about a woman. The woman lives in a future time when women have no rights and are treated as property.

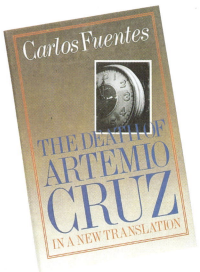

The Death of Artemio Cruz, by Carlos Fuentes, is about an old Mexican millionaire. His life is almost over. In his youth, he fought in the Mexican Revolution, but now he is an old man. He has lost his ideals.

2
- ▶ **Work with a partner. Think of a book you've read or a play or movie you've seen and really enjoyed. Tell your partner what it was about. Try to convince your partner to read it or see it!**

19. I've got a friend who's a cabinetmaker.

John Thomas and Ed Rivera go to the same gym.

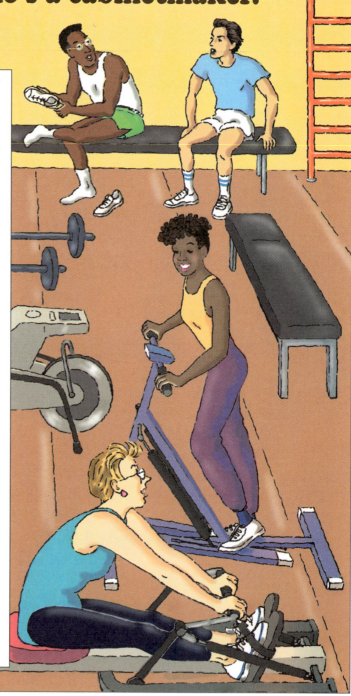

1

John	You look worn out, Ed.
Ed	Yeah, well, we just moved into a new apartment last weekend.
John	You did?
Ed	Yeah . . . and we've been unpacking and cleaning. . . .
John	That sounds exhausting.
Ed	Especially since I work all day and Anita's in school full time now.
John	Carol mentioned something about that. I thought Anita worked at a bank.
Ed	She did, but she was accepted this fall at U.C. Berkeley, so she's taking some time off to get a master's degree.
John	Good for her.
Ed	By the way, John, do you happen to know of anyone who does cabinetwork? We're looking for someone to build kitchen and bathroom cabinets . . . someone reasonable.
John	As a matter of fact, I've got a friend who's a cabinetmaker. He'd do a great job on your apartment, and he's super-reliable.
Ed	Oh, I'd really like to talk to him.
John	I'm not sure if he can do it right away, though. I just happened to have lunch with him today, and he told me the guy he worked with was leaving town. But I'll give you his number, and you can give him a call yourself.
Ed	Hey, it's worth a try. And if he can't do it himself, maybe he can put me in touch with someone who can.

2. Figure it out

Say *True, False,* or *It doesn't say.*

1. A cabinetmaker is someone who builds cabinets.
2. John has been to Ed's new apartment.
3. Ed and Anita don't care how much the cabinets cost.
4. John thinks his friend is someone Ed can count on.
5. John is going to have lunch with his friend next week.
6. John is going to call his friend and ask him to get in touch with Ed.

3. Listen in

Read the statements below. Then listen to another conversation taking place in the gym and choose *a* or *b*.

1. These two women are talking about ___a___.
   a. a book
   b. a play
2. The ___b___ took care of elderly people her whole life.
   a. writer
   b. writer's mother

20. Your turn

Work in groups to figure out what type of book each of these is. Choose a category from the box. Some books may fit into more than one category.

Categories	
fiction	nonfiction
science fiction	autobiography
short stories	mystery novel

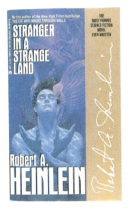

Stranger in a Strange Land
Robert A. Heinlein

The story of a human who was born and raised on Mars. When he visits the planet Earth, he finds the life and people very confusing.

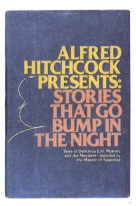

Alfred Hitchcock Presents: Stories That Go Bump in the Night

The ultimate in thrills, mystery, and horror. Stories selected by the great director to make your spine tingle.

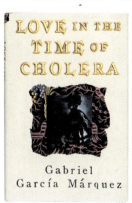

Love in the Time of Cholera
Gabriel García Márquez

After his teenage love marries someone else, Florentino Ariza suffers the anguish of love for over fifty years. But when the loved one becomes a widow, Florentino gets a second chance.

50 Simple Things You Can Do to Save the Earth
The Earthworks Group

An environmental handbook with practical ideas and tips for ordinary people who want to save energy and help preserve the Earth's resources.

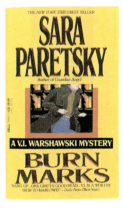

Burn Marks
A V.I. Warshawski Mystery
Sara Paretsky

Private investigator V.I. Warshawski gets caught up in politics and the construction business when her aunt is burned out of her hotel room and disappears.

Totto-Chan: The Little Girl at the Window
Tetsuko Kuroyanagi

A Japanese TV star remembers her childhood.

Discuss these questions in groups.

1. Of these six books, which one would you probably like the most? Why?
2. Of these six books, which one would you probably like the least? Why?
3. What types of books do you usually read?
4. What is the last book you read? What category was it in? Did you like it?

How to say it

Practice the conversation.

A Have you read *The Grapes of Wrath*?

B No, what's it about?

A I'm not sure what it's about.

   I was going to ask you.

21.

Have you read either one of these books?

Stranger in a Strange Land
by Robert A. Heinlein

This entertaining and often shocking novel is designed to make us feel uncomfortable about nearly everything we take for granted. Although techniques of science fiction are used, *Stranger in a Strange Land* might be called a philosophical fantasy or a satire.

Mr. Heinlein uses fictional characters in fictional situations to <u>attack</u> all explanations of the universe based on faith, to <u>undermine</u> the idea of love based on jealousy, and to <u>annoy</u> the materialists and the politicians. He looks at contemporary culture from the nonhuman viewpoint of someone from another civilization. The story is deliberately annoying, and often very funny, but not for people who are easily shocked.

Although he knew it was impossible to be objective, Mr. Heinlein's purpose in writing this novel was to <u>examine</u> every major belief of Western culture, to question each belief, throw doubt on it, and—if possible—to make the <u>opposing</u> view appear a possible and perhaps desirable thing—rather than unthinkable.

The Joy Luck Club
by Amy Tan

In 1949, four Chinese women— drawn together by the shadow of their past—begin meeting in San Francisco to play mah-jongg, invest in stocks, eat dim sum, and "say" stories. They call their gathering the Joy Luck Club.

Nearly forty years later, one of the members has died, and her daughter has come to take her place, only to learn of her mother's lifelong wish— and the tragic way in which it has come true.

The revelation of this secret <u>unleashes</u> an urgent need among the women to reach back and remember . . . .

In this extraordinary first work of fiction, Amy Tan writes about what is lost— over the years, between generations, among friends— and what is saved.

1. **Read these descriptions from two book jackets. Which of the two novels do you think might be based on the author's life experiences?**
2. **Would you like to read either one of these books? Which one? Why?**
3. **Look at the words that are underlined in the descriptions. Match the words with their definitions.**

   1. attack   a. let loose
   2. undermine   b. look at closely
   3. annoy   c. disturb
   4. examine   d. weaken
   5. appear   e. assault
   6. unleash   f. look like

4. **Look at the following adjectives. Which ones are usually positive? Which are usually negative?**

   entertaining   unthinkable
   extraordinary   funny
   shocking   tragic
   annoying   desirable

5. **Write a short description of a book you have read. Give some idea of what the book is about without giving away too much! Make your description interesting, so your reader will want to read the book.**

PREVIEW

FUNCTIONS/THEMES	LANGUAGE	FORMS
Talk about your class or group Make a decision with someone Talk about exceptions	Is everybody here? Everyone but Ana (is). Everyone's here except Ana. What should we have for dinner? Anything is fine with me. Anything but pizza.	Indefinite compounds with *except* and *but*
Report a conversation	He said not to wait for him. She said to wait for her.	
Make plans	How does Wednesday at ten sound? I'm busy all day. I'm busy the whole week. I work every Wednesday.	*The whole*, *all*, and *every* with time expressions
Discuss your plans	I won't be able to make it. I might not be able to make it. I wish I'd known earlier.	
Ask for information	Do you happen to know John's phone number? Not offhand, but I can look it up for you in my address book.	

Preview the conversations.

Student A
You have an English exam on Friday, and you want to get together with Student B one evening to study. Suggest a day and time, using your own information. Keep your book closed while you talk.

Student B
You have an English exam on Friday, and Student A suggests a day and time to study together. Look at the page from the appointment book to see if you're free. If you're not, say why. If you're not sure, say you'll let your partner know.

22. I won't be able to make it.

Some coworkers have organized a company volleyball team and are meeting to decide when to hold practice.

Joan Let's see, who's missing?

Greg Carol's going to be late. She said not to wait for her. She's free every evening except Wednesday.

Joan Is everybody else here?

Stan Everyone except John is.

Joan Does anyone know if he's coming?

Maria Oh, I ran into him this morning. Something came up and he can't make it. But he said to call him and let him know what we've decided. Any evening but Monday's O.K. with him.

Joan So, that leaves Tuesdays, Thursdays, and Fridays.

Peter Tuesdays and Fridays are out for me.

Maria Couldn't we do it on the weekend? We could start this Saturday.

Greg This Saturday isn't good for me. I'm busy all afternoon.

Stan And I'm busy the whole day. In fact, I'm already busy every Saturday this month.

Beth Why don't we meet right after work on Thursday?

Greg That's fine with me.

Peter We could order a pizza.

Stan Please, anything but pizza.

Greg So, will everyone be able to come this Thursday at about six?

Stan Wait! I won't be able to make it. I have a dentist appointment at 5:30.

Greg Could you possibly change it to some other day?

Stan Well, I'll try, but I might not be able to. I wish I'd known earlier. It took me weeks to get that appointment.

Greg So Thursday it is. Does anyone happen to know John's phone number?

Joan I can look it up for you in my address book.

Figure it out

1. Listen to the conversation and say *True*, *False*, or *It doesn't say*.

1. Everyone is at the meeting except Carol.
2. John isn't coming to the meeting.
3. John is free every Monday evening.
4. Everyone is free this Thursday at six.
5. Stan doesn't want to get a pizza.
6. Stan will try to change his dentist appointment.

2. Find another way to say it.

1. Who's not here?
2. It's too bad I didn't know before.
3. Only John isn't (here).
4. She said, "Don't wait for me."
5. I met him by chance.
6. Something unexpected happened, and he can't come.
7. I'll try, but I'm not sure I can.
8. I don't care what you order. Just not pizza.

3. Do the sentences in each pair have the same meaning or different meanings? Say *Same* or *Different*.

1. Everyone but John.
   Everyone except John.

2. Every evening.
   All evening.

3. Everyone but John.
   No one but John.

4. The whole day.
   All day.

5. I'm not sure I can.
   I might not be able to.

6. Anything is O.K. with me.
   Nothing is O.K. with me.

23. Anything but pizza.

1 ▶ Listen to the three possible conversations and practice them with a partner.
▶ Work with a small group. Ask and answer questions about your class, using the questions in the box or your own questions.

A Is everybody here today?

B Yes, everyone's here. **B** Everyone but/except Ana (is). **B** Everyone's here except/but Ana.

Some questions

Is everybody/everyone here today?
Do you know everybody's/everyone's name in the class?
Did you know everyone/everybody before you took this class?
Did you get all of the *Figure it out* items right?
Have you been to every class so far?

Use *everyone* or *everybody* to refer to a whole group of people.
Use *every one* or *all of them* to refer to a whole group of things.

2 ▶ Listen to the conversation about a picnic and check (√) the foods that the speakers decide on.

___ salad
___ hamburgers
___ cookies
___ spaghetti
___ sandwiches

3 ▶ Study the frames: Indefinite compounds with *except* and *but*

Everybody	**but** John came. came **except** John.
Anyplace	**except** the library is O.K. **but** the library is O.K.
Anyone	**but** Sue can give you directions. can give you directions **except** Sue.
Any day	**except** Tuesday is fine. is fine **but** Tuesday.

everybody = everyone
anyplace = anywhere
anyone = anybody

Indefinite compounds with *any* have a different meaning in affirmative and negative statements.
  He eats anything but pizza. = Pizza is the only thing he doesn't eat.
  He doesn't eat anything but pizza. = Pizza is the only thing he eats.

4 ▶ Listen to the three possible conversations and practice them with a partner.
▶ Act out similar conversations, using the questions in the box and your own ideas.

A What should we have for dinner?

B Anything is fine with me.
A Then how about spaghetti?

B Anything but pizza.
A Then how about spaghetti?

B Actually, I don't want to have anything. I'm not hungry.

Some questions

What should we have for dinner?
Where should we go tonight?
When should we study for the English test?
Who should we invite over tomorrow night?

5 ▶ **Rewrite the sentences in brackets [ ], using indefinite compounds with *except* or *but*.**

1. **A** Were there a lot of people at the meeting?
   B [Only Jane didn't come.]
   Everyone except Jane came.

2. **A** Did everyone come to the meeting?
   B [John was the only person who wasn't there.]

3. **A** When do you want to have lunch together?
   B [Monday's the only day I'm not free.]

4. **A** Where would you like to eat?
   B [It doesn't really matter, but just not at Charlie's.]

5. **A** Have you traveled a lot in South America?
   B [No, the only place I've been to is Brazil.]

6. **A** Can someone give me directions to the library?
   B [Sue's the only one who can't give you directions.]

REPORT A CONVERSATION

6 ▶ **Listen to the two conversations and select the message that goes with each one.**

7 ▶ **Listen to the conversation and practice it with a partner.**
▶ **Act out similar conversations, using the information in the box and the pictures.**

A Do you know if John's coming home for dinner?
B He'll be late. He said not to wait for him.

> John said, "Don't wait for me." = John said not to wait for him.
> Ana said, "Wait for me." = Ana said to wait for her.

You're not sure if . . .

your brother John is coming home for dinner.
your friend Gina is coming to town for the class reunion on Sunday.
Mark is going to be at the meeting this afternoon.
Elena is going to the movies with you and your partner.

24. I'm busy all day.

1 ▶ Andrew and Carol are planning a time to get together. Listen to the conversation and put an *X* on the calendar next to the times when they can't meet.

▶ When can Andrew and Carol meet?

Thursday	Friday	Saturday	Sunday
Day	*Day* ✗	*Day*	*Day*
Evening	*Evening*	*Evening*	*Evening*

2 ▶ Listen to the conversation and practice it with two other classmates.

▶ Act out a similar conversation. Try to find a time when you and your classmates can study together.

A When should we meet?
B Let's meet in the morning. How does Wednesday at ten sound?
A That's fine with me. What about you, Terry?
C I can't make it. I'm busy the whole day.
B Then why don't we meet . . .?

I'm busy *the whole* day/*all* day. = I'm not free *that* day.
I'm busy *every* day. = I'm not free *any* day.

Some objections

	the whole day.
	all day.
I'm busy	this whole week.
	all this week.
	every morning this week.

I work all day Wednesday.
I can't make it any afternoon but Thursday.

3 ▶ Study the frame: *The whole, all,* and *every* with time expressions

	the whole	morning.
	all	day.
I'm busy		week.
	every	morning this week.
		week this month.
		Tuesday.

When referring to a week, month, or year, you may also say:

I'm busy *this whole* week.
I'm busy *all this* month.

4 ▶ Karen calls up Short Cuts Hair Salon to make an appointment for a haircut. Complete the conversation with *the whole, this whole, all,* or *every.*

▶ Listen to a possible conversation.

A I'd like to make an appointment for a haircut with Ricardo. Can he see me tomorrow morning?
B Ricardo is busy __all__ morning tomorrow. In fact, he's pretty busy _whole_ week. Let's see . . . how about Wednesday at ten? *(the)*
A I work _every_ Wednesday until noon, and this week I'm also busy __all__ afternoon. I'm free _whole_ day this Thursday, though. *(all)*
B Ricardo is off _every_ Thursday.
A Does he have any openings next Monday?
B Yes, he's free _whole_ afternoon. *(the)*
A I'd like to make an appointment for Monday at four, then.

36 Unit 4

DISCUSS YOUR PLANS

5 ► **Complete the conversation with the sentences in the box.**
► **Listen to check your work.**

Bob We're having a meeting Wednesday at four. Can you be there, Sue?

Sue _____

Bob Great. How about you, Tom?

Tom _____

Bob That's too bad.

Tom _____

Bob Well, how about you, Jan?

Jan _____

Bob O.K., but as soon as possible, please.

> No, I won't be able to make it.
> Sure, I'll be there.
> I might not be able to make it. I'll have to let you know.
> I wish I'd known about the meeting earlier.

> Use *be able to* instead of *can* after modal verbs such as *will*, *might*, *may*, and *should*.

► **Imagine you are planning an event in the future. Act out similar conversations with classmates, using the information in the box.**

> We're having . . .
>
> a meeting.   an office party.
> a (play) rehearsal.   volleyball practice.

ASK FOR INFORMATION

6 ► **Listen and match each conversation with the picture it describes.**

7 ► **Listen to the conversation and practice it with a partner.**
► **Act out similar conversations, using the information in the boxes.**

A Do you happen to know John's phone number?
B Not offhand, but I can look it up for you in my address book.

> Do you happen to know . . .
>
> John's phone number?
> the capital of Chile?
> what *rehearsal* means?
> the country code for Brazil?

> I can look it up in . . .
>
> my address book.
> the atlas.
> the dictionary.
> the phone book.

8 ► **Work with a partner. Use the pictures and information in exercises 6 and 7. Ask and answer questions about information you would like to know.**

Do you happen to know the country code for Poland?

25. Not to change the subject . . .

Lou is telling his friend Andy about Kate, who he's hired to replace Bill.

1

Lou   There's something about Kate. . . . It's very hard to say no to her. You know, when I hired her, I didn't even know her last name. I knew nothing about her except that *she* said she did good cabinetwork.

Andy   Well, does she?

Lou   First-class. But that whole first day, I kept thinking of all the questions I wished I'd asked her.

Andy   Like her last name.

Lou   Right. And I still know practically nothing about her. When I ask her about herself, she changes the subject.

Andy   Where did she learn cabinetwork?

Lou   I guess from experience. She says she's been making cabinets on and off since high school.

Andy   Not to change the subject, but doesn't our waitress look like she could be a dancer?

Lou   Possibly. Why?

Andy   Well, it's just that now any time I see someone who looks like a dancer, I wonder.

Lou   Wonder what?

Andy   Haven't you been reading about the "dancer crimes"? Those people who've been writing bad checks and picking pockets and stealing purses? They're always described in the same way—they look like dancers. . . . It's been in all the papers.

2. Figure it out

Say *True, False,* or *It doesn't say.*

1. Lou found out Kate's last name before he hired her.
2. Kate went to school to learn cabinetmaking.
3. When Lou interviewed Kate, he asked her a lot of questions.
4. Kate doesn't seem to want to talk about herself.
5. The "dancer criminals" have been found by the police.

3. Listen in

Read the two descriptions below. Then listen to the man and woman who are dancing and choose the description that summarizes their conversation.

1. Something is going to happen on Tuesday. The man won't be there because he didn't find out about it soon enough.
2. Something happened on Tuesday. The man wasn't there, but all of the people who live in his building were.

26. Your turn

Read about the sports and games below. Do you like to play or watch any of them?

1. **Volleyball** is played on a rectangular court divided across its width by a high net. Two teams, usually made up of six players each, face each other across the net. Players use their hands to hit a large ball back and forth over the net. One team serves the ball. The opposing team must return the ball within three hits. The serving team scores a point if the opposing team fails to return the ball or hits it out of bounds. If the serving team fails to return the ball over the net, the other team gets the serve. The team that scores fifteen points with at least a two-point lead wins the game.

2. **Soccer** is played on a large rectangular field with a goal at each end. Two teams, made up of eleven players each, try to move a large ball across the field into the opposing team's goal in order to score. A goalkeeper is stationed at each goal to try to prevent the ball from entering the goal. Only the goalkeeper can pick up and throw the ball; everyone else must kick or use another part of the body to move the ball. The team with the most goals at the end of the game wins.

3. **Tennis** is played on a rectangular court divided across its width by a low net. There are two types of tennis games. The singles game is played by two people, with one person on each side of the net. The doubles game is played by four people, with two people on each side of the net. Players use a racket to hit a small ball over the net. A player scores when the opponent cannot return the ball or hits the ball out of bounds. Players with the most points win a game. Those who win the most games win a set. Players who then win the most sets win the entire match.

4. **Chess** is played by two people who sit on opposite sides of a checkered chessboard. Each player starts the game with sixteen pieces (an "army") set in fixed positions on the board. There are six different kinds of pieces, each one allowed to move across the board in a certain way. Players take turns moving their pieces to try to capture the opponent's pieces. The object of the game is to trap the opponent's principal piece, the king, into a position where it cannot escape. When this happens, the advancing player says "Checkmate." If the opposing player cannot find an escape for the king, the first player wins the game.

Discuss the following in small groups and then compare your answers with classmates.

1. How many people in your group like to play each of these sports and games? How many like to watch them?
2. Which of the sports and games use a ball? Which ones are played only with the hands? Which ones are played with other parts of the body? Which ones use a bat, racket, or other instrument? Which one is played sitting down?
3. Think of other sports and games you know. Answer the questions in number 2 for those sports and games.
4. Describe a sport or game you enjoy playing or watching (something different from the four on this page). Explain how it is played and scored. Is there always a winner?

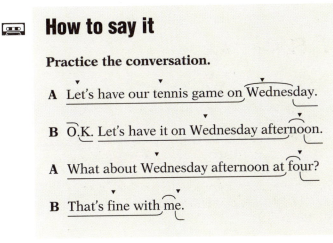

How to say it

Practice the conversation.

A Let's have our tennis game on Wednesday.

B O.K. Let's have it on Wednesday afternoon.

A What about Wednesday afternoon at four?

B That's fine with me.

27.

HEALTHWATCH

How much exercise do you think people need in order to stay healthy? What kind of exercise is best?

How much exercise do we really need?

Ellen and David are committed to their workouts at the health club. They both go every day after work and spend at least one hour doing vigorous exercise, alternating tough aerobics classes with working out on the machines and lifting weights. Both are in shape and feel fit. They believe in the motto "No pain, no gain."

Andy and Pam are sitting in front of the television and watching yet another commercial for the local gym. It all seems overwhelming—going to the gym, working up a sweat, even finding the time. Neither one is an athlete, nor do they really care to learn a sport now.

Are you more like Ellen and David or Andy and Pam? Or do you fall somewhere in between? We all know

that exercise is important in keeping the body healthy and reducing the risks of disease. It also cuts down on stress and protects the body's immune system. But for many people, the word *exercise* conjures up hours of boring, strenuous activity. Recently, however, scientific studies have found that health benefits can be achieved with non-strenuous exercise.

This is very encouraging news for all those people who thought they had to be athletes or work as hard as athletes to make exercise worth it. The new guidelines say that every adult should do at least 30 minutes of moderate activity most days of the week. And these 30 minutes can even be broken down into smaller segments during the day. The important thing is to be consistent and make exercise part of your daily life.

There are many ways to achieve this without buying expensive equipment or joining a health club. Walking is one of the best ways to get exercise. Try to go for a walk after lunch or dinner to boost your metabolism and work off some calories. If possible, walk all or part of the way to work or school. Use the stairs instead of the elevator whenever you can. Gardening, raking leaves, and dancing are also good activities. (However, walking to the coffee or vending machine doesn't count!) As for sports, even if tennis or golf don't appeal to you, hiking and cycling can be relaxing and beneficial too.

Remember, you can be serious about exercise without taking it too seriously!

Read the article about exercise and health. Then take the "fitness test" below to see if you're getting enough exercise. How did you score?

RATE YOUR FITNESS LEVEL

Give yourself the appropriate points for each of the following activities that apply to you.

1. In an average day, I climb _____ flights of stairs.
- **a.** 1 to 5 — 1 point
- **b.** 6 to 10 — 2 points
- **c.** more than 10 — 4 points

2. I lift, carry, or shovel _____ hour(s) a day.
- **a.** 1 — 3 points
- **b.** 2 — 5 points
- **c.** 3 — 7 points
- **d.** 4 — 9 points
- **e.** 5 or more — 12 points

3. I have a desk job but leave my desk more than six times an hour.
1 point

4. I do housework or gardening about _____ hours a week.
1 point for each hour

5. My job requires me to be on my feet and moving _____ hours a day.
- **a.** 1 — 2 points
- **b.** 2 — 3 points
- **c.** 3 — 4 points
- **d.** 4 or more — 6 points

6. My job requires that I stand for _____ hours a day.
- **a.** less than 4 — 0 points
- **b.** 4 — 1 point
- **c.** 6 — 2 points
- **d.** 8 — 3 points

7. I take several short walks or at least one long walk every week, for a total of _____ miles.
2 points for each mile

8. I am a parent of a preschool child who is _____ .
- **a.** at home with me all day — 5 points
- **b.** at home with me half the day — 3 points
- **c.** at home at night — 1 point
(Add 50 percent of points for each additional child.)

9. I play light sports (like softball or volleyball) or go dancing _____ hours a week.
1 point for each hour

How did you score?
- **10 or more points:** Chances are good that you're getting a sufficient amount of physical activity each day, even if you are not engaged in a formal exercise program.
- **5 to 9 points:** You're in fair shape, but you can do much better.
- **0 to 4 points:** You're a couch potato. Try to build more activity into your life.

Review of units 1-4

1 ▶ John and Tina Ross are visitors from out of town, attending a computer software conference. John calls their friends Aki and Sumiko Tanaka. Complete the conversation with the tag questions and rejoinders in the box.
▶ Listen to check your work.

You did?	have you?
You are?	are you?
You don't?	don't you?

Aki So, how long have you been in town?
John We arrived Tuesday night.
Aki *You did ?* Why didn't you call us sooner?
John Well, we've been at the conference every minute. But listen, we'd really like to get together with you and Sumiko. You're not busy this weekend, _____
Aki As a matter of fact, we don't have any plans.
John _____ That's great. How does dinner on Saturday night sound?
Aki Sounds good to me. Say, you and Tina like seafood, _____
John Yes, very much.
Aki Well, there's a terrific new seafood restaurant called Overboard. You haven't been there yet, _____
John No, not yet. But look, *we're* taking *you* out.
Aki _____ Well, that's really nice of you. What time should we meet?
John Oh, about 7:00 . . .

2 ▶ While they're at dinner, the Rosses tell some of their favorite jokes. Complete each joke with *so* or *such*.
▶ Try to think of some other jokes on your own. Tell your jokes in groups.

There's a man down the street who has ___ big feet that when it rains, he lies down and uses them as umbrellas.

I snore ___ much and ___ loud that I used to wake myself up. But now I sleep in the next room and I don't hear a thing.

Have you heard about Will Knott? He's ___ lazy that he signs his name *Won't*.

Last winter, the cow caught ___ a bad cold that she gave ice cream instead of milk.

3 ► Unfortunately, while the Rosses were out, burglars broke into their hotel room. Read the newspaper article about what happened and change the words in brackets [ ] to the passive without an agent.

The Sun ✳ *Sunday late edition*

Park Plaza Hotel Burglarized

Last night at the Park Plaza Hotel, [someone burglarized the guest room of Mr. and Mrs. John and Tina Ross]. *Last night at the Park Plaza Hotel, the guest room of Mr. and Mrs. John and Tina Ross was burglarized.* The Rosses are staying at the Park Plaza Hotel while attending a conference at the Convention Center. [Someone broke into their room] between 6:30 and 10:00 P.M. on Saturday night while the Rosses were at dinner with friends. A hotel security guard noticed that the door to the Rosses' room was ajar just after 10:00 P.M., and [someone at the hotel reported the break-in to police within minutes]. [The burglars took no cash] because the Rosses hadn't left any in the room. [They stole some small pieces of costume jewelry], however. [No one knew their precise value.] The Rosses were upset, of course, but Mrs. Ross was philosophical. She said, "At least [they took nothing of real value]. And the most important thing is that [they harmed no one]." The management of the hotel is cooperating with the police in their investigation.

4 ► Read this article, which appeared in the "Living Section" of the same newspaper.

S U R V E Y : WHAT ARE YOUR PASSIONS?

WHAT DO YOU ENJOY DOING THE MOST?

Peter Wong
Working out—jogging, weightlifting, whatever. Exercising makes me feel great, especially after work. And it's very calming too.

Lynn Harris
Taking photos. I enjoy taking all kinds of pictures—of people, of scenery, of just about anything.

Jack Blade
Eating. I enjoy eating good food, especially organic food. The energy you get from food comes from the earth.

WHAT DO YOU DISLIKE DOING THE MOST?

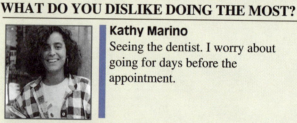
Kathy Marino
Seeing the dentist. I worry about going for days before the appointment.

Don Fisher
Getting my car repaired. No matter what I bring it in for, they always tell me there's something *else* wrong that I didn't know about before.

Liz Ryan
Taking tests. I've always disliked taking tests, no matter what kind—even vision tests! I just freeze up.

► Work with a partner. Find out the two things your partner enjoys doing and dislikes doing the most.

► Compare your answers with your classmates' answers. What are the most popular and the least popular activities for the class?

The most popular activity is . . .
The thing our class enjoys doing the most is . . .
The least popular activity is . . .
The thing our class dislikes doing the most is . . .

5 ▶ **Are you doing the kind of work you really want to do or studying what you're best at? How well do you know yourself? Try to identify your strengths and weaknesses and your likes and dislikes by completing the following sentences.**

1. I've always enjoyed . . .
   I've always enjoyed working with my hands.
2. I've always disliked . . .
3. When I was younger, I used to enjoy . . .

4. I think I'm good at *ler*
5. I'm not very good at . . .
6. I find . . . easy.
7. I have a hard time . . .
8. I find . . . interesting.
9. I find . . . boring.

10. I always look forward to . . .
11. I want to work with people who . *are*
12. I'd like to be someone who *is*
    kreative

6 ▶ **Answer these questions.**

1. Think about the jobs you've had. What are the things you enjoyed most about your jobs? Least?
2. What's the most interesting thing you've done in the last month?
3. What three things are most important to you in a job?

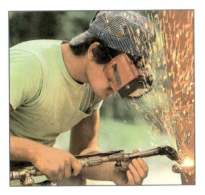

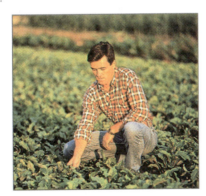

I enjoyed . . .

7A ▶ **Student A follows the instructions below.**
▶ **Student B follows the instructions on page 44.**

Student A Imagine you were just offered a new job. (You can use the jobs in the list or your own ideas.) You're not sure, however, that the job is right for you. Tell your partner what type of job it is and then ask for advice. Share your answers to exercises 5 and 6 with your partner to give him or her a better idea of your likes and dislikes.

Start like this:
A *I was just offered a job as a(n) . . . , but I'm not sure I should take it.*

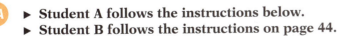

SOME JOBS
a sales manager
an administrative assistant
a chef
a language teacher
a travel agent
a telephone operator
a carpenter
a computer specialist
an exercise instructor
a tour guide
a driver
a waitress/waiter

7B ▸ **Student B follows the instructions below.**
▸ **Student A follows the instructions on page 43.**

Student B   Your partner was just offered a new job but can't decide whether to accept it. Discuss his or her answers to exercises 5 and 6. If you don't think your partner is the right kind of person for the job, try to figure out a better occupation for him or her. Use the expressions in the box or your own ideas.

Start like this:
A *I was just offered a job as a (n) . . . , but I'm not sure I should take it.*
B *Well, do you enjoy . . . ?*

> Why don't you apply for a job as a . . . ?
> You're good at . . .
> They probably want someone who . . .

8 ▸ **Read the statements below. Then listen to Deborah and Carl talk about their jobs. Try to figure out what each of them does and complete the statements. Choose from the occupations in the box.**

1. Deborah is a _____ .
2. Carl is a _____ .

> flight attendant
> pilot
> window washer
> salesperson
> office worker
> waiter/waitress

9 ▸ **Listen to the first part of each conversation and choose the best response.**

1. a. Great! It was one of the nicest vactions I've ever taken.
   b. How about you?

2. a. You will?
   b. You did?

3. a. I've lived here for two years.
   b. I like it a lot.

4. a. I guess you're not used to staying up so late.
   b. I guess you used to stay up late.

5. a. I have a hard time learning languages too.
   b. I'm lucky. I've always found languages easy.

6. a. It was discovered in 1898.
   b. It was discovered by Pierre and Marie Curie.

7. a. I have a friend who does a lot of baby-sitting.
   b. I have a friend who's looking for someone to baby-sit.

8. a. Anyone but Charlie.
   b. Anything but chicken.

9. a. I'll be there. I'm busy all morning.
   b. I won't be able to make it. I'm busy all morning.

10. a. Not offhand. But I can look it up in my address book.
    b. Not offhand. But I can look it up in the dictionary.

P R E V I E W

FUNCTIONS/THEMES	LANGUAGE	FORMS
Tell about a past experience Express duration	We went camping in the mountains last week. During the trip, we had a flat tire. While we were at the concert, someone broke into our house.	*While* vs. *during*
Resume a conversation	Now, what was I saying?	
Talk about your life	I was born in Singapore. I grew up in Hong Kong. I lived there for seventeen years	
Express a wish Talk about imaginary situations	If I had more time, I'd travel. Where would you go? I think I'd go to Africa. What would you do if no one answered the phone?	Contrary-to-fact conditionals
Ask for and give information about objects and places	What delicious cheese! Where is it made? It's made in Switzerland. This building was built in 1776.	The passive in the present and past
Talk about where products are made or produced	Cars are manufactured in Japan. Coffee is grown in Brazil.	

Preview the conversations.

Japanese woodblock print

What interesting prints! Where are they from?

They're woodblock prints. They're made in Japan.

What a nice sweater! Where's it from?

It was made in Ecuador.

Ecuadorean sweater

Do you know of any interesting crafts or products from different countries? Where are they made? Can you describe them?

U N I T 5 • L E S S O N S 2 8 — 3 5

Unit 5 **45**

28. Where are they made?

Debbie and Mike Johnson are browsing at the Small World craft shop in Monterey, California.

A

Debbie Johnson What a wonderful painting!

Helen Silva I love that one, too. It was painted by a young Brazilian artist.

Debbie You seem to have a lot of things from Brazil.

Helen Well, my husband's Brazilian, and I lived there for twenty years. Our son was born and brought up in Rio.

Debbie Really? How long have you been back in the States?

Helen A year now.

B

Mike Johnson Do you like this sweater? It's from Ecuador.

Debbie Mmm, it looks so nice and warm.

Mike Hey, look at those fabulous prints. Where are they made?

Helen Those are woodblocks. They're made in Japan. They're copies of famous Japanese works of art.

Mike They're really nice.

Helen What do you folks do?

Mike I work for a printing company, and Debbie's a physical therapist.

Helen Oh, really? I was a physical therapist before I got married.

Antonio Silva Excuse me, Mom, you have a telephone call.

Helen Will you excuse me for just one moment? . . . (*A few minutes later*) I'm sorry. Now what were we talking about?

Mike You were saying that you used to be a physical therapist.

Helen Oh, yes. In fact, I met my husband while he was in the hospital as a patient. He was a student at San Francisco State University, and he broke his leg during one of his vacations.

Debbie Do you ever miss physical therapy?

Helen Oh, sometimes. If I had more time, I'd have a private practice. But things are so busy at the shop.

Debbie Well, if I had more time, I'd travel.

Helen Where would you go?

Debbie I think I'd go to Africa.

Figure it out

1. Listen to the conversations and say *True*, *False*, or *It doesn't say*.

1. Helen's son grew up in Brazil.
2. The woodblocks in Helen's shop are original works of Japanese art.
3. Helen and her husband met while they were patients in the same hospital.
4. Helen would like to have a physical therapy practice, but she doesn't have time.
5. Debbie has never been to another country.

2. Do the sentences in each pair have the same meaning or different meanings? Say *Same* or *Different*.

1. I lived there for twenty years.
   I lived there twenty years ago.
2. How long have you been back?
   When did you return?
3. What do you folks do?
   What are you folks doing here?
4. He broke his leg during his vacation.
   He broke his leg while he was on vacation.
5. I think I'd go to Africa.
   I'm thinking about going to Africa.

29. During the trip . . .

1 ▶ Listen to David and Louisa talk about their vacation. Then check (√) the pictures that show some of the things that happened.

2 ▶ Complete the conversation about David and Louisa's trip.

Friend So, how was your vacation?
David Oh, we really enjoyed it, but a few things went wrong.
Friend What happened?
Louisa Well, while we were at the airport, _____ .
Friend That's terrible!
Louisa Then, during the trip, _____ .
Friend Gee, you really had some bad luck.
David It wasn't *all* bad. _____ during the trip.
Friend Well, that's good!

3 ▶ Listen to the two possible conversations and practice them with a partner.
▶ Act out similar conversations, using the information in the box and the pictures below.

A We went camping in the mountains last week.

B Oh, really? Did you have fun?

A We had a great time. But during the trip, we had a flat tire.

A We had a great time. But while we were on our way there, we had a flat tire.

We went camping in the mountains last week. We ate at a new French restaurant. We went to a jazz concert.	
During . . .	While . . .
the trip,	we were on our way there,
the meal,	we were at the restaurant,
the concert,	we were at the concert,

. . . we had a flat tire.

. . . all of the lights went out.

. . . someone broke into our house.

4 ▶ **Study the frame:** *While* **vs.** *during*

I didn't do much	**while**	I was on vacation.	◀	*while* + clause
	during	my vacation.	◀	*during* + noun phrase

5 ▶ **Complete the expressions with** *while* **or** *during*. **Then make up sentences about yourself, using these expressions.**
   ▶ **Compare your sentences with a partner.**

1. <u>During</u> my last vacation   *During my last vacation, I went to visit my family.*
2. _____ I was growing up
3. _____ my childhood
4. _____ I was on my way to class
5. _____ the last class

6 ▶ **Work with a partner. Describe a vacation or a trip you've taken. Did anything interesting happen during the trip? Did anything happen while you were away? Describe your experience in as much detail as you can.**

RESUME A CONVERSATION

7 ▶ **Someone interrupts you while you are talking about your trip. Go back to the conversation with your partner.**

A Now, what was I saying?/Now, what were we talking about?

B You were telling me that during your trip . . .

B You were saying that during your trip . . .

30. I was born in Singapore.

1 ► **Read the incomplete description below. Then listen to Rick talk about his life and complete the description about him.**

Rick was born in _____, and he lived there for _____ . He was brought up in _____ . He spoke _____ and _____ at home and _____ at school. His parents wanted him to become _____, but Rick dreamed of being _____ . He studied at _____ and then he went to _____ . However, he also took _____ classes and continued _____ as a hobby. One day, a friend asked him to display his work at _____ . Rick did, and eventually he decided he really wanted to be _____ more than _____ . By then, even his parents knew it was the right decision.

2 ► **Listen to Rick's life story again. Work with a partner. Close your book and retell his story in your own words.**

3 ► **Tell your partner about your life experiences. Use some of the expressions below.**

A *I was born in Singapore.*
B *Did you grow up there?*
A *No, my parents moved when I was six weeks old. I grew up in Hong Kong. I lived there for seventeen years. . . .*

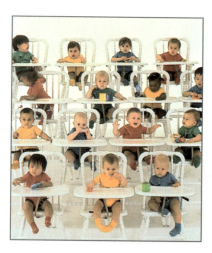

Some life experiences	
I was born in . . .	I was brought up by . . .
I lived there for . . .	I finished school in . . .
We moved when . . .	I started working in . . .
I grew up in . . .	I got married in . . .

31. If I had more time, I'd travel.

1
► Listen to the conversation and practice it with a partner.
► Act out similar conversations. Discuss what you would do if you had more time. Use the information below or your own ideas.

A If I had more time, I'd travel.
B Where would you go?
A I think I'd go to Africa.

I'd = I would

If I had more time, I'd . . .

travel.
read more.
fix up my house/apartment.
learn to play an instrument.
get more exercise.
learn to speak another language.

Which one would you learn?
Where would you go?
What kinds of things would you read?
What would you do exactly?

2
► Study the frame: Contrary-to-fact conditionals

| What **would** you **do** | if you **had** more time? | If I **had** more time, | I'd **travel**. |
| Where **would** you **go** | if you **traveled**? | If I **spoke** Spanish, | I'd **go** to Peru. |

In a contrary-to-fact conditional, we are imagining a situation that is not true.

If I had more time = I don't have more time.
If I spoke Spanish = I don't speak Spanish.

3
► Complete the conversations using the verbs in parentheses.
► Listen to check your work.
► Practice the conversations with a partner.

1. **A** What would you do if you _____ (have) all the time in the world?
   B I think I _____ (travel) to other countries.
   A Which countries _____ (visit)?
   B I _____ (start) in Argentina, then I _____ (go) to Chile, Brazil, and Peru. . . . In fact, I _____ (try) to see every country in South America.

2. **A** What would you do if you _____ (have) lots of money?
   B First, I _____ (give) a big contribution to AIDS research and other charities. Then I _____ (buy) a big house with a swimming pool!
   A _____ (quit) your job?
   B Well, I have two jobs, so I guess I _____ (quit) one of them!

► Have similar conversations. Student A: Ask the first question from each conversation above. Student B: Answer with your own ideas. Take turns asking and answering.

4
► Work with a partner. Take turns asking and answering questions for each situation.

Student A Imagine you were in these situations. What would you do?

Student B Continue the conversations by asking your partner more questions.

1. Imagine you went to a restaurant and ordered a meal. Then you realized your wallet was missing. What would you do?
   A *I'd explain the situation to the manager.*
   B *What would you do if the manager didn't believe you?*
   A *Then I'd call a friend and ask him or her to come to the restaurant.*
   B *What would you do if no one answered the phone?*
   A *I'd . . .*
2. Imagine that someone you disliked invited you to a party. What would you do?
3. Imagine that your boss asked you to work all night. What would you say?
4. Imagine that you saw a crime in the street. What would you do?

32. Where is it made?

1
- ▶ Listen to the conversation and practice it with a partner.
- ▶ Act out similar conversations about the things in the pictures and about objects in your classroom.

A What delicious cheese! Where is it made?
B It's made in Switzerland.

What delicious cheese! Where is it made?
It's made in Switzerland.

What a beautiful picture! Where was it taken?
It was taken in Portugal.

What delicious oranges! Where are they grown? They're grown in Florida.

2 ▶ Study the frames: The passive in the present and past tense

Active				Passive			
Subject (agent)	Verb	Object		Subject	Form of *be*	Past participle	
Farmers	grow	oranges	in Florida.	Oranges	**are**	**grown**	in Florida.
They	make	cheese	in Switzerland.	Cheese	**is**	**made**	in Switzerland.
Workers	built	this building	in 1776.	This building	**was**	**built**	in 1776.
My father	took	these pictures	in Portugal.	These pictures	**were**	**taken**	in Portugal.

same tense

When it is unnecesary to name the agent or if the agent is unknown, it is omitted in passive sentences.

3 ▶ Read this page from a guidebook about San Francisco. Then rewrite it, changing the words in brackets [ ] from active to passive.

pLACes of inTEResT in San Francisco, California

[They started **Golden Gate Park** in the 1870s.] _Golden Gate Park was started in the 1870s._ [They changed it from a wasteland to a beautiful park] with lakes and exotic trees from all over the world. Walk through the 1,000-acre park and stop at the **Japanese Tea Garden.** [They serve tea at the teahouse daily.]

Mission San Francisco de Asis is one of the oldest buildings in San Francisco. [They opened it in October 1776.] [They brought many of the pictures and books in the mission from Spain and Mexico.] [They display old manuscripts and other objects from the early days of the mission in a small museum.]

Alcatraz Island, in San Francisco Bay, was once a prison but is now part of the Golden Gate National Recreation Area. [They imprisoned famous criminals, such as Al Capone and Machine Gun Kelly, there.] [They offer tours of the prison.] You can buy tickets at Fisherman's Wharf, where the tour departs, but [they recommend advance ticket purchases, especially during the summer].

On the way to Alcatraz Island, be sure to stop at **Fisherman's Wharf** and walk along the waterfront, enjoying the colorful sights and smells of the markets, restaurants, and shops. A specialty is sourdough bread—[they bake it fresh daily].

4 ▶ **Work with a partner. Talk about where different products are made, produced, manufactured, raised, and grown. Use the map and your own knowledge.**

A *Cars are manufactured in Japan.*
B *Where else are they made?*
A *They're made in many countries, such as . . .*

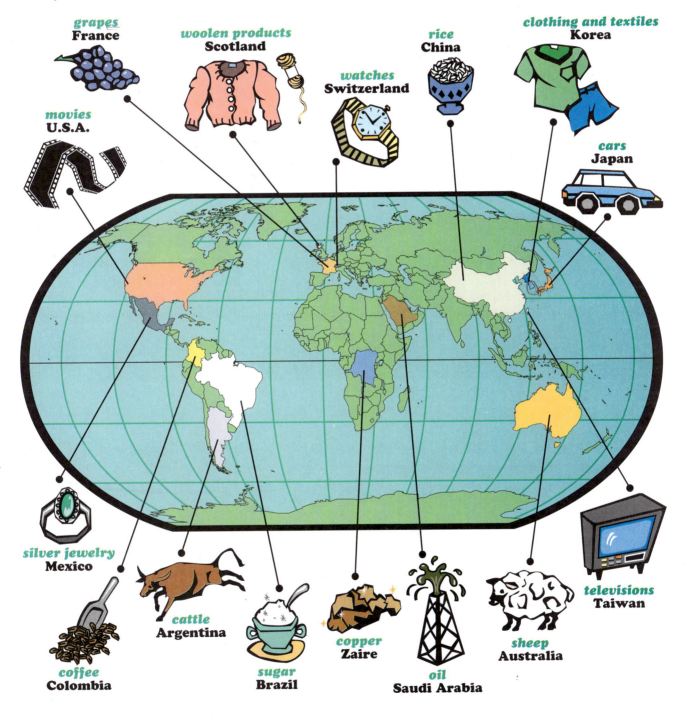

grapes
France

movies
U.S.A.

woolen products
Scotland

watches
Switzerland

rice
China

clothing and textiles
Korea

cars
Japan

silver jewelry
Mexico

coffee
Colombia

cattle
Argentina

sugar
Brazil

copper
Zaire

oil
Saudi Arabia

sheep
Australia

televisions
Taiwan

5 ▶ **Name some other products not listed above. Where are they made?**
▶ **Name some things that are produced in your country.**

33. But isn't it too valuable . . . ?

Lou and Kate have started working for the Riveras, who are showing them their most valuable possession.

1

Kate	What a beautiful mask!
Anita	Oh, thank you. We got it while we were traveling in Africa a few years ago.
Ed	Yeah, the minute we saw it we knew we had to have it.
Anita	Don't you think it'll look perfect in this kitchen, once it's done?
Kate	Yes, it'll be very striking. But isn't it too valuable to be hanging in the kitchen? I'd be worried someone would take it.
Anita	Well, as it turns out, it *is* fairly valuable. But when people break into apartments, they're more interested in TV sets and CD players than they are in masks.
Lou	Unless, of course, they're professionals— the kind who steal from museums.
Anita	Now who would think of looking in our apartment for a museum piece? I guess I believe you have to take chances in life.
Ed	Speaking of chances, I'd better run, or there's a good chance I'll miss my bus. Have a good day.
Lou	You too. Nice meeting you.

2. Figure it out

Say *True, False,* or *It doesn't say.*

1. The Riveras got the mask during a trip to Australia.
2. Anita is planning to hang the mask in the kitchen.
3. The mask is worth a lot of money.
4. Ed and Anita have a CD player and a TV set.
5. Anita doesn't think many people steal museum pieces from apartments.
6. Anita worries a lot about robberies.

3. Listen in

Anita, Lou, and Kate continue their conversation. Read the statements below. Then listen to the conversation and say *True* or *False.*

1. Ed and Anita lived in San Diego during their childhood.
2. Ed and Anita visit Ed's parents often.

34. Your turn

Look at the pictures of crafts from different countries. Then, work in groups to figure out the answers to the questions for each object. Use the information in the boxes. If you have trouble, you may look up the answers on page 165.

1. What is it?
2. Where was it made?
3. What is it made of?

ceremonial mask   glass/Venice, Italy
aboriginal bark painting   silver/Mexico
wine glass   wool/Navajo Indian reservation,
rug   Southwestern U.S.A.
jewelry   wood/Africa
                bark/Australia

a. *silver Mexico*

b. *wood Africa*

c. *wooll Navajo*

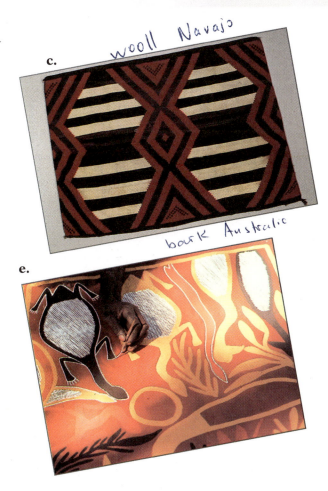

d. *glass Venice*

e. *bark Australia*

Discuss these questions in groups.

1. Does your country have crafts that are similar to the ones in the pictures?
2. What other kinds of crafts are made in your country?

How to say it

Practice the conversation.

A If I had more time, I'd travel.

B Where would you go?

A If I had enough money, I'd go to Africa.

35. The Art of Japanese Woodblock Printing

Woodblock prints are illustrations made from a carved block of wood and printed on paper. They were first used in Japan in the 1600s to illustrate books. When readers became more and more interested in the illustrations for their artistic value, publishers hired skilled artists to create prints which could be sold separately. By the end of the seventeenth century, techniques were developed to produce many copies of a print from the same woodblock, making this fine art available to the general public.

Look at the picture of a Japanese woodblock print. How do you think it was made?

The most famous Japanese woodblock prints were made during the 1700s and 1800s. The styles were unique to Japan. Scenes from everyday life or the theater, beautiful women, and landscapes were often the subjects of these prints. The Japanese name *ukiyo-e*, meaning "pictures from the floating world," is used to describe the famous woodblock prints from this era: This refers to images of fleeting moments of pleasure, amusement, and entertainment captured by the artists. Later, European artists, particularly painters of the French Impressionist School, admired and were influenced by the bold colors and unusual designs of these Japanese woodblock prints.

Portrait by Utamaro

Making a woodblock print has three major stages: cutting, inking, and printing. First the artist takes a block of soft wood, usually pine, and cuts away parts of the wood with a sharp tool. The design is the part of the wood that is left uncut and upraised. Next the design is coated with ink, and a sheet of paper is placed over it. Rubbing the paper then transfers the ink from the woodblock to the surface of the paper. For different colors, different blocks of wood are used, one for each color.

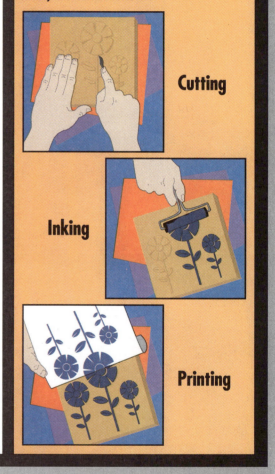

Cutting

Inking

Printing

1. Read the article. Then say *True* or *False*.

1. Woodblock prints are always one-of-a-kind paintings.
2. Woodblock prints are made by carving an image out of a block of wood.
3. Some famous Japanese woodblock prints illustrate scenes from everyday life.
4. The French Impressionist School of painting came before Japanese woodblocks.
5. Woodblock prints can be made only in black and white.

2. Can you describe how another art or craft is made? Tell the class about it, and, if possible, bring a sample to class.

PREVIEW

FUNCTIONS/THEMES	LANGUAGE	FORMS
Offer to do someone a favor Ask a favor of someone	Can I get you anything while I'm out? Do you think you might go by a post office? I could. What would you like? Could you have them weigh this package?	
Have something done	I'd like to have this film developed. He'd like to have them develop this film.	The causative *have*
Make a request	Would you mind mailing some letters? No, not at all. Could you get me a book of first-class stamps? Sure.	Noun compounds
Go shopping	I might as well get a tie.	

Preview the conversations.

Student A
You're going downtown to run some errands. Tell your partner which store or place you're going to. Student B will ask you a favor. Agree or refuse.

Student B
Ask your partner to do you a favor, but only if it's not out of the way or too much trouble.

36. Just one more thing . . .

Richard is going to run some errands on his lunch hour. He asks some of his coworkers if they need anything.

A

Richard I'm going downtown to run some errands. Can I get either of you anything while I'm out?
Tina Do you think you might go by a post office?
Richard I could. What would you like?
Tina Could you have them weigh this package? Oh, and while you're there, could you get me a book of first-class stamps?
Richard Sure. I'd be glad to.
Tina I'll go get some money.
Richard Don't worry about it. You can pay me when I get back.
Keith If you happen to go by a drugstore, could you have this prescription filled for me?
Richard Sure. No problem.
Keith But don't bother if it's inconvenient. Here's a twenty-dollar bill. I'm sure that'll be more than enough. Oh, and would you mind mailing these letters?
Richard Not at all.
Keith Just one more thing . . . could you drop off this film at a camera shop?
Richard Sure, if I have time.
Keith I'd really appreciate it. I've been meaning to take it in for a month.

B

Salesperson Can I help you?
Richard I'd like to have this film developed.
Salesperson Just write your name and address here, please.
Richard Oh . . . it's for someone else. I don't know his home address. I'll have to make a phone call and come back.
Salesperson O.K. Will there be anything else?
Richard Yes, while I'm here, I might as well get a roll of film—color prints, 24 exposures.
Salesperson Here you are.
Richard How much do I owe you?
Salesperson $5.35 with tax.
Richard By the way, is there a drugstore near here?
Salesperson The closest one would be on Fourth and Main. It's about a ten-minute walk.
Richard And what about a post office?
Salesperson There's one on Fifth and Main, not too far from the drugstore.

Figure it out

1. Listen to the conversations and say _True, False,_ or _It doesn't say._

1. Richard wasn't planning to go to the post office.
2. Tina gave Richard money for the stamps.
3. Keith needs some medicine from the drugstore.
4. The medicine will cost more than twenty dollars.
5. Keith took his pictures a few days ago.
6. Keith's roll of film had 24 pictures.
7. The nearest drugstore is about ten minutes from the camera shop.
8. The post office is a long way from the drugstore.

2. Choose _a_ or _b._

1. Could you have them _____ this package?
   ✓ a. weigh
   b. to weigh

2. You can pay me _____ I get back.
   a. while
   ~ b. when

3. Here's a twenty- _____ bill.
   ✓ a. dollar
   b. dollars

4. Would you mind _____ these letters?
   ✓ a. mailing
   b. to mail

5. I'd like to have this film _____ .
   a. develop
   ∨ b. developed

6. _____ I'm here, I think I'll get some film.
   ✓ a. While
   b. When

7. The drugstore is ten _____ from here.
   a. minute
   b. minutes

37. Can I get you anything?

1 ► Listen to the conversation. Check (√) the places where Rose is going.
► Listen again. How many things do Rose's friends ask her to do?

2 ► Listen to the conversation and practice it with a partner.
► Act out similar conversations, using the pictures and information.

A I'm going downtown. Can I get you anything while I'm out?
B Do you think you might go by a post office?
A I could. What would you like?
B Could you have them weigh this package?
A Sure. I'd be glad to.

Maybe he's going by a post office. He could have them weigh this package.

Maybe she's going by a camera shop. She could have them develop this film.

Maybe he's going by a shoe-repair shop. He could have them put new heels on these shoes.

Maybe he's going by a photocopy shop. He could have them copy these papers.

3 ► Work with a partner. Act out conversations similar to those in exercise 2.

Student A Say where you're going. Offer to do your partner a favor.
Student B Ask your partner to do something for you.

A *I'm going .... Can I get you anything?*
B *Do you think you might go by ...? Could you ...?*

HAVE SOMETHING DONE • THE CAUSATIVE *HAVE*

4
- ▶ **Listen to the conversation and practice it with a partner.**
- ▶ **Act out similar conversations, using the information in the boxes.**

A Can I help you?
B I'd like to have this film developed.
A Will there be anything else?
B Yes, while I'm here, I might as well get a roll of film.

I'd like to have . . .
this film developed.
this package weighed.
this prescription filled.
new heels put on these shoes.

I might as well get . . .
some shoe polish.
a roll of film.
a book of stamps.
some aspirin.

5 ▶ **Study the frames: The causative *have***

Active construction

He'd like to	have	me you him her us them	Verb	
			develop	this film.
			take	a photograph.

Passive construction

He'd like to	have		Past participle
		this film a photograph	**developed**. **taken**.

A passive construction often follows *have* when it is unnecessary to name the agent.
  I'd like to *have* this film developed (by someone).

Compare:
Could you *have* her *call* me?
Could you *ask* her *to call* me?

6
- ▶ **Complete the conversations, using *have* and an active or passive form of the verb in parentheses.**
- ▶ **Listen to check your work.**

1. **A** I'm going into town. Is there anything you need?
   B Do you think you might go by a drugstore? I need to <u>*have a prescription filled*</u> (fill) .
   A O.K., sure.

2. **A** May I speak to Sylvia, please?
   B I'm sorry, she's not here right now.
   A Could you (call) _____ ? This is Ted Block.
   have her call me
3. **A** My camera is broken. I have to *have it* _____ (fix). *fixed*
   B There's a good camera shop on Main Street.

4. **A** I'm going to the dry cleaner's. Can I drop off anything for you?
   B Yes. This dress has a big coffee stain. I really need to *have* _____
   this dress (clean). And say, while you're there *I'd like to have* the hem on *it cleaned*
   this skirt is falling down. They always do alterations
   for me. Could you _____ (fix)? *have this skirt fixed*
   it.
   A Sure, no problem.

7 ▶ **Talk to your classmates. Give examples of some things you need to have done.**

I need to have my hair cut.
I have to have my car serviced.

I need to have my hair cut.

38. Would you mind mailing these letters?

1 ▶ John is going to run some errands. His friends ask him to do some things for them. Listen to the conversation and write down the requests they make. Check (√) *Yes* or *No* to show if John agrees to the requests.

Request	Yes	No
• Mail letters	√	
•		
•		
•		
•		

2 ▶ Listen to the conversation and practice it with a partner.
   ▶ Act out similar conversations, using the information in the boxes.

A I'm going to the post office.
B While you're there, would you mind mailing these letters?
A No, not at all.
B Here's a ten-dollar bill. Thanks a lot.

I'm going . . .
to the post office.
into the kitchen.
to the dry cleaner's.
to get a slice of pizza.

Would you mind . . .
picking up my suit?
bringing me an apple?
mailing these letters?
getting me one, too?

Other ways to say it
Could you mail these letters?
Would you mail these letters?

3 ▶ Study the frame: Noun compounds

A store where they sell groceries is a **grocery store**.
A shop where they do repairs on shoes is a **shoe-repair shop**.
A bill worth ten dollars is a **ten-dollar bill**.

Sometimes the two words of a noun compound are written as a single word (*bookstore, drugstore*). You should check your dictionary for the correct spelling. Notice that the modifying nouns of compounds such as *shoe-repair shop* and *ten-dollar bill* are hyphenated.

4 ▶ Answer these questions, using noun compounds. Then make up similar questions of your own. (The answers must have noun compounds.)

1. What do you call a bill worth twenty dollars?   *A twenty-dollar bill.*
2. If you take a walk for ten minutes, what do you call it?
3. What's a store where they sell jewelry?
4. What do you call a lamp that sits on a table?
5. What's a weekend that lasts three days?
6. What do you call a teacher who teaches French?
7. What do you call an apartment with two bedrooms?
8. What's a station where you can get on or off a train?
9. What's a catalogue that you use to order things by mail?
10. If you take a break from work for five minutes to have coffee, what's it called?

39. I might as well get a tie.

 1 ▶ Here are some items you can find in a department store. List them under the departments they belong in.

TV set	lamp	children's shoes	dress	bedroom set
women's raincoat	calculator	tie	men's shoes	nail polish
dining set	running shoes	men's socks	refrigerator	earrings
men's suit	eye makeup	chairs	lipstick	men's belt
washing machine	computer table	cordless telephone	headphones	boots
ring	sofa	bracelet	clothes dryer	vacuum cleaner
radio	men's shirt	desk	CD player	blouse
perfume	video game	hiking shoes	necklace	video cassette recorder (VCR)

BASEMENT
Electronics Dept.
TV set

MAIN FLOOR
Cosmetics Dept.

SECOND FLOOR
Shoe Dept.

THIRD FLOOR
Women's Clothing Dept.

FOURTH FLOOR
Men's Clothing Dept.

FIFTH FLOOR
Home Appliances Dept.

SIXTH FLOOR
Furniture Dept.

SEVENTH FLOOR
Jewelry Dept.

2 ▶ Bruce and Nancy are shopping in a department store. Listen to their conversation in the elevator. Write the items they want to buy and which departments they are going to.

3 ▶ Work in groups. Imagine you are looking for a gift for someone. Describe that person to your classmates. They will make suggestions about a gift they think you should buy. You can use some of the items in exercise 1.

A *I need to get a birthday gift for my 15-year-old brother. He really likes computers and videos.*
B *You could get him a video game.*

40. They're quite a pair.

Anita Rivera is talking to one of her professors, Dr. Kim, after class.

1

Dr. Kim That was an excellent paper you wrote, Anita.

Anita Oh, thank you, Dr. Kim.

Dr. Kim I was especially interested in the real-life experience you brought to it.

Anita Oh, you mean my work at the bank?

Dr. Kim Yes, it's excellent when you can relate your university courses to actual job experience.

Anita Hmm, I guess I'd never thought of it that way. Going back to school, I felt a little out of place.

Dr. Kim Really? Why? I think you bring valuable knowledge with you, especially in the field of economics that we're studying.

Anita Well, I'm glad I managed to get the paper done on time. My husband and I just moved into a new apartment, and on top of all the confusion, we've got two cabinetmakers working there. We're having the kitchen and bathroom redone.

Dr. Kim Cabinetmakers? I've been thinking of having some bookcases built in my living room—maybe ones with cabinets. Do you think they might be able to do some work for me?

Anita I'll ask them. They're quite a pair—a young man and woman. She looks more like a dancer than a cabinetmaker.

2. Figure it out

Say *True, False,* or *It doesn't say.*

1. Anita's paper was the best one in the class.
2. Anita has experience working at a bank.
3. Dr. Kim teaches economics.
4. Anita turned in her paper late.
5. Dr. Kim is looking for someone to build bookcases in her living room.

3. Listen in

Dave King and Jill Wong, two of Anita's classmates, are talking after class. Read the questions below. Then listen to the conversation and answer the questions.

1. What is Jill going to do for Dave?
2. What is Dave going to do for Jill?

41. Your turn

Work with a partner. Play these roles.

Part 1

Student A You're going out to run some errands. You have to take care of the items in the picture below. Ask if your partner needs anything.

Student B You have to take care of the items in the picture below. Your partner is going out to run some errands and asks you if you need anything. Find out where your partner is going and make requests. Be considerate, and don't ask your partner to go somewhere inconvenient.

Part 2

Student A You have just arrived at the first store to run the errands from Part 1. Your partner is a salesclerk and will help you.

Student B You are a sales clerk at a shoe-repair shop, a drugstore, a dry cleaner, or a post office. Your partner is a customer. Respond to his or her requests.

How to say it

Practice the conversations.

A Why are you going to the camera shop?

B Because I want to have them develop this film.

A Why are you going to the camera shop?

B Because I want to have this film developed.

42. HOME SHOPPING TV NETWORKS: The Wave of the Future?

Have you ever watched a home shopping program on TV? Can you describe what it's like to shop at home by television?

Have you ever had to decide whether to go shopping or stay home and watch TV on a weekend? Now you can do both at the same time. Home shopping television networks have become a way for many people to shop without ever having to leave their homes.

Some shoppers are tired of department stores and shopping malls—fighting the crowds, waiting in long lines, and sometimes not even finding anything they want to buy. They'd rather sit quietly at home in front of the TV set and watch a friendly announcer describe an item while a model displays it. And they can shop around the clock, purchasing an item simply by making a phone call and charging it to a credit card. Home shopping networks understand the power of an enthusiastic host, the glamour of celebrity guests endorsing their products, and the emotional pull of a bargain.

Major fashion designers, department stores, and even mail-order catalogue companies are eager to join in the success of home shopping. Large department stores are experimenting with their own TV channels, and some retailers are planning to introduce interactive TV shopping in the future. Then, viewers will be able to communicate with their own personal shoppers, asking questions about products and placing orders, all through their TV sets.

Will shopping by television replace shopping in stores? Some industry executives claim that home shopping networks represent the "electronic shopping mall of the future." Yet for many people, going out and shopping at a *real* store is a way to relax and even be entertained. And for many shoppers, it is still important to touch or try on items they want to buy. That's why experts say that in the future, home shopping will exist alongside store shopping but will never entirely replace it.

HandyCam

---

1. **Read the article about home shopping by television and find words or phrases that mean about the same as the ones below.**

1. they can shop at any hour
2. famous
3. supporting
4. the temptation
5. sellers or stores that sell directly to the public
6. TV that you communicate with

2. **Discuss these questions in groups.**

1. What are some reasons why people like to shop at home? What are some reasons why other people prefer store shopping?
2. Have you ever watched a home shopping program on TV? Do you think it's a good way to shop? Why or why not?

PREVIEW

FUNCTIONS/THEMES	LANGUAGE	FORMS
Tell about a past experience	I was reading in bed when I heard footsteps downstairs. He started up the stairs while I was talking on the phone.	The simple past vs. the past continuous with *when* and *while*
Tell a frightening story	It was a cold winter night. It was after midnight when I left the party . . .	
Apologize	I'm sorry if I frightened you.	
Start a conversation Ask for a reason	Haven't we met somewhere before? Why doesn't he write more often?	Negative questions
Refresh your memory	Where did you say you lived?	

Preview the conversations.

Look at the pictures and describe what is happening in each one. Here are some verbs you can use: *yawn*, *wear*, *turn off*, *go*, *get into*, and *come into*. *The woman is yawning. She's turning off the lamp.*

43. I was reading in bed when . . .

Maggie Donovan, whose husband is on a business trip, is in bed. She's alone in the house.

A

Police officer Police.
Maggie (*Whispering*) Hello, I live at 26 Larchmont . . .
Police officer Could you speak up, please?
Maggie I can't talk very loudly. Someone's in my house. He's walking around downstairs.
Police officer Where did you say you lived?
Maggie At 26 Larchmont Terrace.
Police officer Someone will be right there. Don't hang up.
Maggie Oh, no! He's coming upstairs!
Police officer Ma'am?

B

Fred Maggie?
Maggie Oh, Fred. It's you!
Police officer Ma'am?
Maggie (*Talking into phone*) Oh, I'm so sorry. It was my husband. I mean, I'm glad it was my husband. I'm sorry for the inconvenience.
Police officer No problem, ma'am. Good night. (*Hangs up*)
Fred I'm sorry if I frightened you.
Maggie You scared me to death. I thought you were coming home tomorrow.
Fred Well, as it turns out, I got through a day early.
Maggie Why didn't you call?
Fred I wanted to surprise you.

C

Maggie I had the most frightening experience last night.

Susan What happened?

Maggie Well, I was reading in bed at about eleven o'clock when I heard footsteps downstairs. Someone was walking around.

Susan Oh, no! What did you do?

Maggie I called the police. But while I was talking on the phone, the person started coming up the stairs.

Susan Did you see him?

Maggie Yes.

Susan You must have been terrified.

Maggie It was Fred.

Susan Fred! Isn't he out of town?

Maggie He finished his work and came home early.

Susan Doesn't he call when he changes his plans?

Maggie He wanted to surprise me.

Figure it out

1. Listen to the conversations and put the events in order.

___ It turned out to be Fred, Maggie's husband.

___ The person started up the stairs while she was on the phone.

___ Maggie heard footsteps downstairs.

_1_ Maggie was reading a book in bed.

___ Someone came into the house.

___ She was frightened, so she called the police.

2. Find another way to say it.

1. I had a very scary experience.
2. You frightened me terribly.
3. Could you speak louder?
4. Where do you live again?
5. I finished up a day early.
6. But he's out of town, isn't he?
7. I'm sure you were very frightened.

3. Complete each conversation with *a* or *b*.

1. I was reading in bed when I heard footsteps.
   a. What were you doing?
   ✓ b. What did you do?

2. Hi, Maggie. I'm home.
   ✓ a. I thought you were coming home tomorrow.
   b. I think you're coming home tomorrow.

3. I live at 26 Larchmont Terrace.
   ✓ a. Where did you say you lived?
   b. Where did you live?

4. Why didn't you call first?
   ✓ a. I wanted to surprise you.
   b. I wanted to talk to you.

5. What did you do?
   a. I was calling the police.
   ✓ b. I called the police.

44. I heard footsteps.

1 ▶ Listen to the two possible conversations and practice them with a partner.
▶ Act out similar conversations, using the pictures and information below.

A I was reading in bed when I heard footsteps downstairs.
B What did you do?
A I called the police.

A While I was reading in bed, I heard footsteps downstairs.
B What did you do?
A I called the police.

read in bed
hear footsteps downstairs

call the police

walk down the street
grab my purse

run after him

hike through the woods
see a bear

not move a muscle

fry chicken
catch fire

pour water on it

2 ▶ Study the frames: The simple past vs. the past continuous with *when* and *while*.

Past continuous	
I **was reading** in bed	**when** I **heard** footsteps downstairs.
I **was talking** on the phone	**when** he **started** up the stairs.

Simple past	
I **heard** footsteps downstairs	**while** I **was reading** in bed.
He **started** up the stairs	**while** I **was talking** on the phone.

Use the simple past continuous to describe a past event.
I read a book. (I finished the book.)
Use the past continuous to describe a continuous action in the past.
I was reading a book. (I was somewhere in the middle of the book.)
When describing two past events, one of which interrupts the other, use the simple past with the action that interrupts the continuous action.
I was reading a book when I heard a loud noise outside.

3 ▶ **Read the incomplete stories. Put the verbs in parentheses into either the past continuous or the simple past.**
   ▶ **Listen to check your work.**
   ▶ **Finish the stories any way you wish.**

The Visitor

My whole body *was aching* (ache) when I _____ (get) home. I _____ (go) into the bathroom, _____ (get) undressed, and _____ (step) into the hot shower. While I _____ (dry off), the doorbell _____ (ring). I quickly _____ (put on) some clothes. Then, while I _____ (run) down the stairs toward the front door, something very strange _____ (happen) . . . ,

Night of Terror

It was a cold winter night. It was after midnight when I _____ (leave) the party and _____ (start) walking home. It _____ (snow) heavily, and the wind _____ (scream) in my ears. I was the only person around, or so I thought. Suddenly, while I _____ (walk) through a park about a block from my house, I _____ (hear) a low voice behind me. When I _____ (turn around), there, only a few inches from my face, was . . .

4 ▶ **Listen to Vincent describe a bad experience to a friend. Then decide whether each statement is *True* or *False*.**

1. Vincent was waiting to cross the street when he saw a car racing toward him.
2. The traffic light was green when Vincent started to cross the street.
3. While he was crossing the street, the light turned red.
4. Vincent ran to the other side of the street when the light turned yellow.
5. The car was speeding and never slowed down.
6. While the car was speeding toward him, Vincent turned around and jumped back onto the curb.

▶ **Work with a partner. Close your books and retell what happened to Vincent. Use *when* and *while*.**

5 ▶ **Match the pictures with the sentences in the box.**

1. Did I frighten you?   3. Did I seem rude on the phone?
2. Did I make you late?   4. Did I keep you waiting?

6 ▶ **Listen to the conversation and practice it with a partner.**
   ▶ **Act out similar conversations, using the pictures in exercise 5.**

A I'm sorry if I frightened you.
B Oh, that's O.K. Don't worry about it.

45. Haven't we met somewhere before?

1 ▸ These people are at a party. Complete each conversation with a question from the box.
▸ Listen to check your work.

Haven't we met somewhere before?

Yes, I think we met in Santiago last year.

No, it's Don, but you were close!

Yes. As a matter of fact, I'm a news announcer.

Mmm. It really is.

Yes, I did. We were in the same class.

Yes, he just started there.

Haven't we met somewhere before?
Isn't your name Dan?
Doesn't your husband work at Super Software Systems?

Didn't you take English literature last semester?
Isn't the food delicious?
Aren't you on TV?

2 ▸ Study the frame: Negative yes-no questions

Isn't	your name Steve?
Doesn't	Fred call when he changes his plans?

Negative yes-no questions, like tag questions, are used to confirm information, but they can also express some surprise or doubt.
Isn't Fred out of town? (You thought he was, but now you're not sure.)
Doesn't Fred call when he changes his plans? (You're surprised he didn't this time.)

3 ▸ Listen to the two possible conversations and practice them with a partner.
▸ Act out similar conversations, using the questions in the box or your own ideas. Answer with your own information.

A Isn't your last name Mendez?

B Yes, it is.　　　　**B** No, it's Mendel.
A That's what I thought.

Some questions

Isn't your last name . . . ?
Aren't you from . . . ?
Don't you live in . . . ?
Didn't you take a . . . course last year?
Haven't we met somewhere before?

4 ▶ **Study the frame:**
Negative information questions

| Why | **didn't** Thomas Edison go to school as a child? |
| | **aren't** there any houseflies in Alaska? |

5 ▶ Listen to the conversation and practice it with a partner.
▶ Act out similar conversations, using the information in the boxes below.

A Why aren't there any houseflies in Alaska?
B They can't live there because it's too cold.

Some interesting facts	Some interesting reasons
There aren't any houseflies in Alaska.	His first teacher said he was too stupid to learn anything.
People can't sink in the Dead Sea.	They can't live there because it's too cold.
Thomas Edison didn't go to school as a child.	It would form balls that float.
You can't pour water into a cup in space.	It's too salty.

6 ▶ Complete the conversations, using negative yes-no questions.

1. A *Haven't we met before?* You look familiar.
   B Maybe we have. You look familiar, too.
   _____ ?
   A That's right. You helped me with my English homework.

2. A _____ ? It's the last meeting of the year.
   B No, I can't make it, but what about next month? _____ ?
   A They've canceled it. Everyone but us will be on vacation.

3. A We're all out of milk again.
   B _____ ?
   A I did, but Tony drank all of it last night.

7 ▶ Complete the conversations, using negative information questions with *why*.

1. A I haven't heard from my brother in six months.
   B Really? *Why doesn't he write more often?*
   A He hates to write letters.

2. A Why _____ ? It's so late.
   B I've been too busy. I haven't had time for lunch.

3. A Lou won't be able to come over later.
   B That's too bad. _____ ?
   A He has a doctors' appointment.

4. A I'm trying to call Marie, but there's no answer.
   B Really? I know she's there. _____ ?
   A Maybe she just stepped out for a minute.

8 ▶ Listen to the conversation and practice it with a partner.
▶ Act out similar conversations, using the questions below.
▶ Ask your partner more questions, using your own information.

A Where did you say you lived?
B At 26 Larchmont Terrace.

Some questions		When the main verb is in the past, use a past form for the verb that follows, even when you're referring to the present. Compare:	Other ways to say it
Where did you say	your teacher was last term?	Where *do* you *live*?	Where do you live again?
What did you say	you lived?	Where *did* you say you *lived*?	
When did you say	you did?		
Who did you say	you spelled your last name?		
How did you say	your birthday was?		

46. Where did you say you were from?

A few days later, Lou tries to find out a little more about Kate.

1

Lou	Where did you say you were from?
Kate	Actually, I don't think I've ever said. I never know how to answer that question, in fact. We moved around a lot when I was a kid.
Lou	Really? I was brought up in a small town in Ontario and never moved anywhere until I came here. That must have been interesting, living in different places.
Kate	Well, it depends. I had a hard time making friends while I was growing up. We never stayed in one place long enough.
Lou	How come you moved so much?
Kate	My parents changed jobs a lot. It had its advantages, though—lots of excitement.
Lou	You know, one nice thing about cabinetwork is that you don't have to sit in one place. I've always enjoyed physical work.
Kate	I know what you mean. I don't think I could stand working in an office.
Lou	While we're on the subject of work, I've been meaning to tell you that I'll have to leave the Riveras' at three tomorrow. I have to be somewhere at three thirty.
Kate	No problem. I can stay behind and finish up.

2. Figure it out

Say *True, False,* or *It doesn't say.*

1. Lou forgot where Kate was from.
2. Lou thinks it's interesting to live in different places.
3. Kate had a lot of friends when she was a child.
4. Lou enjoys the type of work he does.
5. Kate would like to work in an office.
6. Lou has to leave the Riveras' early because he has a doctor's appointment.

3. Listen in

A man is talking to a police officer on the street near Lou and Kate. Listen to the conversation and choose *a* or *b*.

1. a. The thieves grabbed the man while he was crossing the street.
   b. The thieves grabbed the man after he crossed the street.

2. a. The thieves ran away when the other woman started shouting.
   b. The other woman started shouting after the thieves ran away.

47. Your turn

Look at the pictures below and work in groups to decide what happened in them. Make up a story, putting the pictures in any order you wish. Here are some words you can use: *argue, storm out, thunderstorm, turbulence, frightened, safe landing, relieved, make up.*

kiss and make up.

🔊 How to say it

Practice the conversation.

A Where did you say you lived?

B At 2545 (twenty-five forty-five) Bushnell Drive.

A And what's your phone number again?

B 555-3967 (five-five-five three-nine-six-seven)

UFOs: Fact or Fiction?

Have you ever heard of a UFO (Unidentified Flying Object)? Do you think UFOs are spaceships from other planets, or is there some other explanation for them?

The existence of UFOs (Unidentified Flying Objects) is a source of controversy that often divides people into two separate groups: those who believe that UFOs are the spaceships of intelligent beings from other planets, and those who disagree and believe these sightings have some other explanation. Those in the second group say these sightings could be due to the effects of a distant planet, a weather disturbance, or airplane lights, for example. Another possible explanation is that the people who report the sightings could be imagining what they saw or making up stories to get attention.

Over the years there have been many reports of people seeing mysterious objects in the sky. Sometimes these objects are described as having unusual bright lights. Some people even claim they have been taken on board spaceships by alien creatures. Those who insist they have indeed been abducted by aliens have very strange stories to tell. Most of them share the same experiences such as being approached by creatures with large heads on small bodies with slits for eyes. These people say they have been led onto the spaceships against their will and given examinations and tests. After they are returned home, they might experience anxiety with occasional flashbacks and unusual dreams.

One such mystery happened in 1975 in Arizona. Travis Walton, then twenty-two, was traveling in a truck with a group of men when they suddenly spotted a bright object. They stopped, and when Walton got out to get a better look, a beam of light came down and hit him. His friends were so frightened that they drove off. They saw the light take off into the sky and decided to return with flashlights. They couldn't find any signs of Walton, so they reported him missing.

Five days later, Walton called his sister from a phone booth twelve miles away. He sounded upset and in pain. When he was picked up, he kept talking about awful creatures with horrible eyes that stared at him as they led him onto a spaceship. At one point he found himself on an examination table, surrounded by the aliens. He was terrified and tried to attack the creatures, but they left the room. Frightened, he ran off into another room. He saw other humans there but then passed out. When he woke up, he was lying in the road, and saw the UFO take off. Walton's story has never been proved or disproved. However, Walton has passed a lie-detector test more than once.

Some people who believe they have been abducted by aliens undergo hypnosis to try to "remember" what really happened. But this is not actual proof, for it is possible to "remember" something that was only a dream. Critics say that many people are influenced by UFO stories they have read and then use their colorful imaginations to come up with their own stories and finally convince themselves that these events took place.

Are these people trying to play tricks on us? Are they confused and possibly showing signs of mental problems? Or are some of them telling the truth?

1. **What are the two explanations for UFO sightings? Describe the two different points of view with as many details as you can. (One view is "fact," the other "fiction.")**

2. **Do you believe there is life on other planets? If so, do you think aliens have ever visited the Earth? What makes you think so?**

Review of units 5–7

1 ▶ Complete the jokes with the verbs in parentheses. Use the
simple past or the past continuous.
▶ Tell the jokes to a partner.

1. The students _were waiting_ (wait) at their
desks when Mr. Cogswell _____ (arrive).
He _____ (walk) to the blackboard and
_____ (write) the title of the day's composition:
"The Most Beautiful Thing I've Ever Seen." Most
of the students _____ (think) about what to
write when Clyde Thomas, one of the worst
students in the class, _____ (give) Mr. Cogswell
his paper and _____ (leave) the room. It
_____ (not/take) Mr. Cogswell very long to
read the composition: "The most beautiful thing
I've ever seen was too beautiful for words."

2. When Sue _____ (move) to a new town, she
_____ (meet) Jane, the little girl next door.
Jane _____ (be) younger than Sue, but the two
girls _____ (get along) well together. One day,
while they _____ (play), Sue _____ (ask)
Jane, "Have you lived here your whole life?" "Not
yet," Jane _____ (answer).

3. One day, a man _____ (ride) a horse when he
_____ (pass) a dog on the road. "Good
morning," the dog _____ (say). "I didn't know
dogs could talk," the man _____ (say).
"Neither did I," _____ (say) the horse.

2 ▶ Rewrite the story, changing the expressions in brackets [ ] into
compound nouns.

THE 300-POUND REINDEER

One day, [a reindeer that weighed 300 pounds] *One day, a
300-pound reindeer* walked into [a shop where they serve
coffee], sat down at the counter, and ordered [a dish of ice
cream that cost fifty cents].

When it arrived, he took [a bill for ten dollars] out of his
[purse for change] and put it on the counter. The waiter
didn't think the reindeer knew anything about money and
gave him only a dollar in change.

"You know," said the waiter, "we don't get many reindeer
here. In fact, you're the first one we've ever had."

"Well," said the reindeer, "at nine dollars a dish of ice cream,
you probably won't get many more."

3A ▶ Student A follows the instructions below.
▶ Student B follows the instructions on page 78.

Student A Imagine that you and your partner just met at
a party, but you're both sure that you've met before.
Refresh your memory by asking your partner negative
yes-no questions based on the information below.

We met in Argentina. *Didn't we meet in Argentina?*
We met at a dinner party.
It was during the spring.
We went out for coffee afterwards.
Your last name is Carter.

"Didn't we meet in Argentina?"

"No, we met in Chile."

3B ▶ Student B follows the instructions below.
▶ Student A follows the instructions on page 77.

Student B Imagine that you and your partner just met at a party, but you're both sure that you've met before. Your partner will ask you questions about the first time you met. Answer, using the information below.

We met in Chile. *No, we met in Chile.*
We met at a barbecue.
It was during the summer.
I went right home afterwards.
My last name is _____ (your own last name).

"Didn't we meet in Argentina?"   "No, we met in Chile."

4 ▶ Listen to Mark describe what happened to him last night.
▶ Work with a partner and retell the story, using the pictures.
Use *when* and *while*. You can start like this:

Last night while Mark was walking home from work, . . .

▶ Tell your partner about something frightening that happened to you. (It doesn't have to be a true story!)

5A ▶ Student A follows the instructions below.
▶ Student B follows the instructions on page 79.

Student A Imagine you are going to the places in the pictures. Tell your partner you are planning to run some errands. Your partner will ask some favors. You can agree or refuse.

5B ▶ Student B follows the instructions below.
▶ Student A follows the instructions on page 78.

Student B Your partner is going out to run some errands. You need the following things. Ask your partner to do you some favors.

photocopy these papers

refill this prescription

get a newspaper

shine these shoes

6 ▶ Rewrite the sentences in brackets [ ], using the cues.
▶ Practice the conversations with a partner.

1. **A** [I forgot your last name. What is it?]
   What did you say your last name was?
   B Wolsky.

2. **A** I'm going out for a while.
   B [Are you going by the post office? I need stamps.]
   If you happen . . . , could you . . . ?

3. **A** [Hand me that bag.]
   Would you mind . . . ?
   B Here you are.

4. **A** What can I do for you today?
   B [Repair these shoes, please.]
   I'd like to have . . .

5. **A** Oh! I didn't know you were here.
   B [Did I frighten you? I'm sorry.]
   I'm sorry if . . .

What did you say your last name was?

Wolsky.

7 ▶ Rearrange the words in brackets [ ] to make sentences.
▶ Listen to check your work.
▶ Practice the conversation with a partner.

A I'm going to run some errands. [anything get Can you I ?]
B [mind a up Would newspaper you picking?]
A [all at Not .] I'll be back around 6:00.
B Where are you going?
A [my cut hair going have to I'm.]
B Really? [too short Don't it cut have.]
A I won't. [having too thinking dyed I'm it about.]
B What color?
A Maybe orange.
B Good choice.

8 ▶ Complete each sentence, using the passive voice with the verbs in parentheses.

1. Snacks and soft drinks _are sold_ (sell) in the lobby.
2. Smoking _____ (not/permit) anywhere on the aircraft.
3. Payment _____ (expect) at the time of service.
4. Boarding passes _____ (issue) on the day of the flight.
5. Calls _____ (answer) in the order they _____ (receive).
6. Interest _____ (credit) at the end of each month.

9 ▶ Here are some places to see in Boston. Read the article. Then rewrite it, changing the sentences in brackets [ ] to the passive. Omit the agent when it is unnecessary.

PLACES OF INTEREST IN Boston

[They built **Faneuil Hall** in 1742.] _Faneuil Hall was built in 1742._ [Peter Faneuil gave it to the city of Boston.] [They call Faneuil Hall "The Cradle of Liberty" because they used it as a meeting hall during the American Revolution.] [They still use the first floor as a market.]

The Museum of Fine Arts has Asian, Egyptian, Classical, European, and American paintings and sculpture. [They opened the west wing in July 1981.] [They close the museum on major holidays.]

[Henry Hobson Richardson completed **Trinity Church** in 1877.] [They hold guided tours after the 11 A.M. Sunday service.] [They give free concerts at 12:15 P.M., October 1 to May 30.]

FANEUIL HALL

10 ▶ Listen to the first part of each conversation and choose the best response.

1. a. I took a shower.
   b. I was taking a shower.

2. a. Would you like some stamps?
   b. Would you mind getting me some stamps?

3. a. Could you have her call me, please?
   b. Could you call me, please?

4. a. I'd learn a new language.
   b. I'll learn a new language.

5. a. I'd live in Korea.
   b. In Korea.

6. a. Maybe he's not at home.
   b. Maybe he didn't answer the phone.

7. a. The food is delicious, isn't it?
   b. Yes, it really is.

8. a. Will there be anything else?
   b. I'd like to have this prescription refilled.

9. a. It was made in Brazil.
   b. I'm from Brazil.

10. a. No, not at all.
    b. No, thanks.

FUNCTIONS/THEMES	LANGUAGE	FORMS
Cancel plans Give an excuse	I'm sorry to let you down, but I can't go to the concert tonight. I have too much work to do.	Infinitives after direct objects
Give advice	You'd better give it to her. You'd better not interrupt her.	*Had better* and *had better not*
Ask permission	Would you mind if I opened the window?	
Ask a favor of someone Agree or refuse to do a favor	I'd really appreciate it if you could help me print out my report. I think I can. I wish I could, but I have to work.	
Say thank you	I really appreciate your helping me.	
Discuss arrangements and obligations	What time are we supposed to meet Carla and Rob?	*Be supposed to*

Preview the conversations.

The movie starts at 8:00. Do you want to get a bite to eat first?

Look, I'm really sorry to let you down, but . . .

Student A
You and Student B have plans to go to the movies tonight. Call Student B to confirm your plans.

Student B
You were supposed to get together with Student A tonight, but you have to work late instead. When Student A calls, cancel your plans and explain why.

49. You'd better go without me.

Rita is under a lot of pressure at work. Tim, a coworker, offers to help her out.

A

Tim Rita, your husband just called.

Rita Oh, am I supposed to call him back?

Tim No, he'll call back later. He wanted to tell you that there was a change in plans for tonight.

Rita I'll say! We were planning to go to an outdoor concert, but now I have this report to write. I just found out about it an hour ago, and I have to have it ready tomorrow morning! What am I going to do?

Tim Gee, Rita, don't get so upset. Look, is there anything I can do to give you a hand? Maybe I could help you print out the report and photocopy it.

Rita Oh, I'd really appreciate it if you could, but I don't want you to ruin your evening.

Tim It's no problem. I'm supposed to meet someone at 6:00, but I should be able to change my plans. Look, I know you've been under a lot of pressure, and I just don't want you to quit. . . .

B

Rita Hello?

Steve Hi, Rita. It's me. Listen, Carla and Rob would like to have dinner with us before the concert.

Rita Hmm . . . what time are we supposed to meet them?

Steve At about six.

Rita You'd better go without me. I really wish I could go, but I have too much work to do. I'm writing this report, and it has to be ready tomorrow. My boss is really on my back about it.

Steve Oh, that's too bad. What about the concert?

Rita You'd better not count on me for that, either.

Steve Oh, Rita, not again!

Rita I'm sorry to let you down. But look, my job is on the line here.

Steve O.K., O.K. I'm sorry if I sounded annoyed with you.

Rita That's O.K. I understand. Maybe we're both a little edgy.

Tim I'm just about finished. . . .
   Uh, would you mind if I
   opened this window? It's
   getting stuffy in here.
Rita Not at all. Go right ahead.
   Tim, I really appreciate your
   staying late. I owe you one.
Tim Oh, I'm happy to help you
   out. I'm sure you'd do the
   same for me.
(*Phone rings*)
Rita Maybe that's Steve. I might
   be able to go to the concert
   after all.

Figure it out

1. Listen to the conversations and choose *a* or *b*.

1. a. Rita had plans to go to a concert tonight.
   b. Rita doesn't want to go to the concert tonight.

2. a. Rita has to finish the report by tomorrow.
   b. Rita can't finish the report by tomorrow.

3. a. Tim is going to meet someone at 6:00.
   b. Tim is able to change his plans.

4. a. Tim is doing Rita a favor by staying late.
   b. Tim has to stay late anyway.

2. Find another way to say it.

1. There sure is (a change in plans)!   *I'll say!*
2. May I open this window?
3. I'm sorry to disappoint you.
4. Thanks so much for staying late.
5. I have to write this report.
6. Is there any way I can help you?
7. Does he expect me to call him back?

3. What do these sentences imply? Choose *a* or *b*.

1. We're supposed to go.
   a. We've arranged to go, but we might not go.
   b. We're definitely going.

2. I should be able to change my plans.
   a. I don't think I can change my plans.
   b. I think I can change my plans.

3. I have a report to write.
   a. I'm going to write the report.
   b. I've already written the report.

4. I really appreciate your staying late.
   a. I hope you're staying late.
   b. You're staying late.

5. I really wish I could go.
   a. I can't go.
   b. I'll let you know if I can go.

6. Would you mind if I opened the window?
   a. The window is open.
   b. The window is closed.

50. I have too much work to do.

1 ► Listen to the conversations. In each one, someone has to cancel plans. What plans do they cancel and what excuses do they give? Match each conversation with the correct picture. Then write the excuse under each picture.

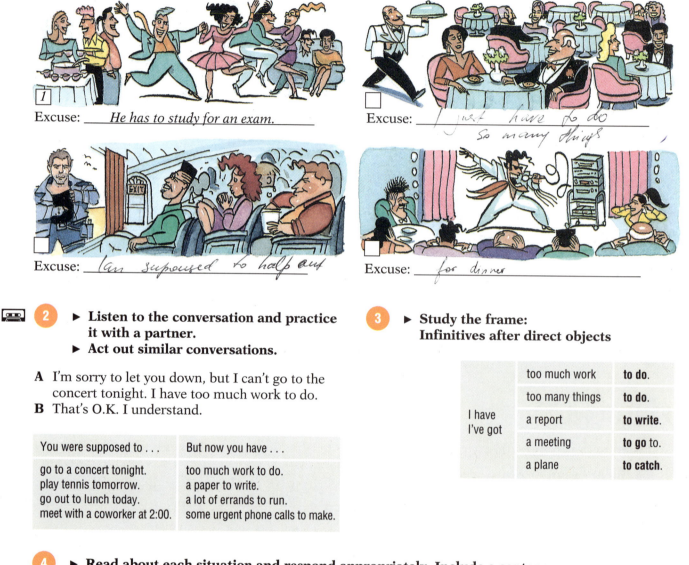

Excuse: *He has to study for an exam.*

Excuse: I just have to do so many things

Excuse: I an supposed to help out

Excuse: for dinner

2 ► Listen to the conversation and practice it with a partner.
► Act out similar conversations.

A I'm sorry to let you down, but I can't go to the concert tonight. I have too much work to do.
B That's O.K. I understand.

You were supposed to . . .	But now you have . . .
go to a concert tonight.	too much work to do.
play tennis tomorrow.	a paper to write.
go out to lunch today.	a lot of errands to run.
meet with a coworker at 2:00.	some urgent phone calls to make.

3 ► Study the frame:
Infinitives after direct objects

	too much work	**to do**.
	too many things	**to do**.
I have I've got	a report	**to write**.
	a meeting	**to go** to.
	a plane	**to catch**.

4 ► Read about each situation and respond appropriately. Include a sentence with an infinitive after the direct object in each response.

1. Your plane leaves in an hour, and you're about to leave for the airport. A neighbor stops you and starts a long conversation. Give an excuse. *I'm sorry, but I'd better go. I have a plane to catch.*

2. You haven't written to six of your friends in months, and you feel bad about it. Someone asks you how you're going to spend your evening. Say what your plans are.

3. You're reading an article for school, and you're almost finished. You've just started the last page when a friend knocks on your door. Explain the situation.

4. You forgot to mail your bills this morning. You're in a car with a friend who's driving by a post office. Make a request.

5. You have a big exam tomorrow, but you haven't started studying for it yet. You were planning to go to the movies tonight with a friend. Cancel your plans.

GIVE ADVICE • *HAD BETTER* AND *HAD BETTER NOT*

5 ▶ **Listen to the conversation between Peggy and Carl. Check (√) the things that Carl decides to do.**

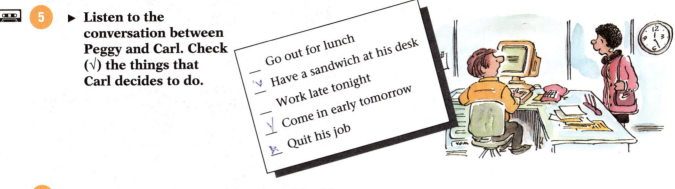

___ Go out for lunch
_√_ Have a sandwich at his desk
___ Work late tonight
_√_ Come in early tomorrow
_✗_ Quit his job

6 ▶ **Study the frames:** *Had better* **and** *had better not*

Affirmative statements		
You	**'d better**	give it to her.

Negative statements			
You	**'d better**	**not**	interrupt her.

'd better = *had* better

7 ▶ **Listen to the conversation and practice it with a partner.**
▶ **Act out similar conversations, using the situations and advice with** *had better* **or** *had better not.*

Some situations
There's an urgent fax for Karen but she's on the phone
We have to leave for the concert no later than seven.
Pablo doesn't know about our change in plans.
I haven't started writing my paper.

Some advice
Don't put it off too long.
Go without me.
Don't interrupt her.
Try to get hold of him.

A There's an urgent fax for Karen, but she's on the phone.
B You'd better not interrupt her.

ASK PERMISSION

8 ▶ **Listen to the two possible conversations and practice them with a partner.**
▶ **Act out similar conversations.**

A Would you mind if I opened the window? It's getting stuffy in here.

B Not at all. Go right ahead.   **B** Well . . . I'd rather you didn't.

Would you mind if I . . .	
opened the window?	I'm having trouble concentrating.
turned off the air conditioner?	It's really warm in here.
turned on the air conditioner?	It's getting stuffy in here.
turned down the radio?	It's getting chilly.

Other ways to say it
Do you mind if I open the window?
May I open the window?

9 ▶ **Work with a partner. Imagine you are in the following situations. Ask your partner permission to do something, using** *"Would you mind if I . . . ?"* **Then give a reason. Your partner will respond.**

1. You're driving a car at night, and your partner is a passenger. You're getting sleepy and think you'd better stop for coffee.
2. You are a dinner guest at your partner's home. Now it's time for dessert. You've had a wonderful meal, but you're really full and think you'd better skip dessert.
3. You are sitting next to your partner on an airplane. You've left your newspaper at home. Your partner has finished reading his/her newspaper, and you'd like to read it.
4. You're a guest at your partner's home. The TV set is off, but you're anxious to know the latest soccer scores.

51. I'd appreciate it if you could help me.

1 ▶ Listen to the conversation between Johnny and his mother. What favors does she ask him to do? Does he agree or refuse? Write the favors in the box. Then check (√) *Agree* or *Refuse* for each.

Favor	Agree	Refuse
• *Take out the garbage.*	√	
•		
•		

2 ▶ Listen to the two possible conversations and practice them with a partner.
▶ Act out similar conversations. Student A: Use the information in the box to ask your partner some favors. Student B: Agree or refuse. If you refuse, give an excuse.

A I'd really appreciate it if you could help me print out my report tonight.

B I think I can. I'm supposed to meet someone at 7:30, but I should be able to change my plans.

B I wish I could, but I have to work.

Could you help me . . .

print out my report?
move?
fix my bicycle?
put up some shelves?
with my math homework?

3 ▶ Ask a classmate to help you do something. Your partner will agree or refuse.
Could you help me find this word in the dictionary?
I'd really appreciate it if you could help me do the homework.

SAY THANK YOU

4 ▶ Listen to the conversation and practice it with a partner.
▶ Act out similar conversations with a partner, using the information in the box.

A I really appreciate your printing out this report for me.
B I'm happy to do it. I'm sure you'd do the same for me.

I really appreciate your . . .

printing out this report for me.
driving me to class.
helping me clean up.
doing the dishes.

5 ▶ Read the thank-you note. Then write a thank-you note to someone who has done something for you. Compare it with your classmates' notes.

Dear Terry,

I really appreciate your helping me with my résumé. Your advice was very helpful, and I feel more confident about my job search now that I've had the benefit of your experience. Maybe someday I can return the favor.

Yours sincerely,
Pat

52. What time are we supposed to be there?

1 ▶ **Study the frames:**
Be supposed to

Present tense yes-no and information questions		
Am I **Are** we	**supposed to**	call Steve back? pick up Amy?
Where When	**am** I **are** we	**supposed to**	meet Carla and Rob? send this letter?

Be supposed to vs. *have to*		
I **'m supposed to**	meet someone later.	▶ I've arranged to meet someone later, but I might not.
I **have to**		▶ I'm going to meet someone later.

2 ▶ **Listen to the conversation and practice it with a partner.**
▶ **Act out similar conversations, using the information below.**

A What time are we supposed to meet Carla and Rob?
B At six . . .

Some obligations

You and your partner are supposed to meet Carla and Rob for dinner, but you don't know what time or where.
Your brother, Rob, is supposed to be in town next week, but your sister hasn't told you when he's coming or how long he's staying.
You're supposed to send a report out at work, but your boss hasn't told you who to send it to.

Meet Carla and Rob in front of the Rose Café at 6:00 P.M. on

I'll be in town on business from September 10th to September 15th. Please tell everyone in the family.
Love,
Rob

MEMO
Send this week's report to:
Mr. Alvarez
Ms. Wells

3 ▶ **Helen is trying to organize a meeting. Some people definitely can't come and some of them aren't sure yet. Restate the information, using a form of *be supposed to* or *have to* in your answers.**

1. Bob has a doctor's appointment that he can't change.
   Bob has to go to the doctor.
2. Bill and Sue have another meeting to go to, and they can't change their plans.
3. Jim and Barbara have plans to go out of town, but they'll see if they can leave a day later.
4. Carol wishes she could come, but she teaches then.
5. Don is planning to go shopping with a friend, but he'll try to change the day.
6. Jane has an invitation to a friend's house, but she might be able to go another day.

4 ▶ **Work in groups. Think of some things you are supposed to do but don't always manage to do. Then report to the class.**

Boris is supposed to do the laundry every Thursday. He usually does it, but sometimes he forgets.

53. Something's come up.

Lou is getting ready to meet some friends Thursday evening when the phone rings.

1

Lou Hello?

Kate Hello, Lou. This is Kate.

Lou Kate! What's up?

Kate Lou, I'm not going to be able to come to work tomorrow. . . . Something's come up.

Lou Are you O.K., Kate? You sound funny.

Kate No, everything's O.K. Really. But I appreciate your concern, Lou. I hope to be back at work on Monday.

Lou Well, thanks for letting me know.

Kate There's one more thing, Lou. I . . . uh . . . well, I was wondering if you could pay me early.

Lou Gee, I don't know Kate.

Kate Lou, I promise to be back on Monday, bright and early. I really need the cash now.

Lou Well, O.K. I can stop by in the morning . . . if you tell me where you live.

Kate I'd really appreciate it if I could pick up the money from you tonight.

Lou Well, the problem is I'm supposed to meet some friends in twenty minutes. I guess I could call them . . .

Kate No, I don't want you to change your plans. Isn't there somewhere you could leave the check?

Lou Let me think. . . . You know where they deliver magazines, under the mailboxes? I'll put the check in an issue of *Sports Illustrated*. . . .

2. Figure it out

Choose *a* or *b*.

1. a. Kate can't work tomorrow because she's going out of town.
   b. Kate doesn't say why she can't work tomorrow.

2. a. Lou is a little worried when he finds out that Kate can't come to work.
   b. Lou doesn't seem concerned at all.

3. a. Kate doesn't know when she'll return to work.
   b. Kate plans to return to work on Monday.

4. a. Lou knows Kate's address.
   b. Lou doesn't know where Kate lives.

5. a. Kate will pick up her paycheck.
   b. Lou will take the paycheck to Kate's house.

3. Listen in

Just as Lou is going out the door, the phone rings again. Read the statements below. Then listen to the conversation and say *True* or *False*.

1. Anita wants Lou and Kate to come to her house at eight the next morning.
2. Lou is going to call Kate.
3. Lou says that he and Kate will be there at eight o'clock.
4. Anita tells Lou what she and Ed want to talk to him about.

54. Your turn

Read about the Gitlins' situation.

1. **At lunchtime, Andy Gitlin bought some expensive theater tickets to celebrate his parents' fiftieth wedding anniversary on Saturday, February 20th.**

2. **That evening, Andy's wife, Stephanie, called Andy's parents to invite them to the play. The senior Gitlins were delighted and immediately accepted the invitation.**

3. **The next day, Stephanie received an invitation for the same night from her company president.**

As your new president, I would like to extend to you on behalf of my wife and me an invitation to join us for dinner at our home on Saturday, February 20 at 7:00. We hope you and your guest will be able to attend. I look forward to becoming better acquainted with all of you.

Charles F. Anderson

R.S.V.P. by February 10

Tel. 555-0784

Consider this information.

1. Stephanie is being considered for a promotion to vice president of the company.
2. Andy started his current job only six months ago, and now his company is downsizing. He could lose his job sometime soon, in which case Stephanie's salary would be the family's only income.
3. Andy's mother has recently had a serious illness.
4. Andy's parents disapproved of Stephanie for many years after they got married. They've only recently started to get along with her.

Now work in groups and discuss these questions.

1. What are some reasons Stephanie and Andy should go to the play? The company dinner?
2. What decision should Stephanie and Andy make? Why?
3. If Stephanie and Andy decide to go to the dinner, what should they say to Andy's parents?

Work with a partner. Imagine that you're in the Gitlins' situation. You've just read the invitation and are trying to decide what to do. Act out the conversation between Stephanie and Andy.

🔊 How to say it

Practice the conversation.

A I'm not going out for lunch today.

   I have a report to write.

B I'm not going out for lunch, either.

   I have some phone calls to make.

55. 🔘 # QUIZ: What Kind of Job Is Best for You?

Before you take the quiz, read through it quickly. Then complete exercise 1. When you have finished, take the quiz and analyze your score.

by Jane Sherrod Singer, M.A.

This quiz is designed to give you an overall view of your career aptitudes and interests. Please answer the following questions YES or NO. There are no right or wrong answers.

1. Do you enjoy games that require concentration, such as chess or bridge?

2. If you had to take a course in school, would you select astronomy, biology, or math rather than history, philosophy, or art appreciation?

3. Do you usually remember specific facts you have read or heard?

4. If you had your choice, would you rather do a few things very well than many things fairly well?

5. Do you keep records, such as budgets, a telephone book of personal and business numbers, and lists of things to do?

6. Do you keep up with new vocabulary in the fields of science, technology, and medicine?

7. As a child, did you enjoy taking things apart to see what made them work?

8. Were mathematics and sciences easy for you in school?

9. If you were given a paid month's vacation to France, would you spend the time exploring Paris or some other place in depth rather than seeing all you could of the entire country?

10. Do you usually prefer novels to factual material, such as biographies, business publications, or scientific books and articles?

11. Do you usually prefer to spend your spare time with people rather than reading, or pursuing a hobby you do by yourself?

12. Do you dislike eating alone?

13. Do you enjoy new people, places, and things?

14. Do you select clothing that has flair and commands attention?

15. Can you do several things well at the same time?

16. Do you usually feel at ease and sincerely interested when you are with people who are much older or younger than you?

17. Do you feel you make lasting friendships easily?

18. Do you enjoy learning new facts and skills even though you cannot necessarily use them at the time?

HOW TO ANALYZE YOUR SCORE:

1. If you have many more YES answers to the first nine questions than the last nine, you are probably someone who enjoys jobs which require patience and attention to detail (scientist, laboratory researcher, accountant, artist).

2. If you have many more YES answers to the last nine questions than the first nine, your greatest strength is in working with people (politician, lawyer, actor, waitress, athlete).

3. If your YES answers are fairly evenly divided between the first nine and the last nine questions, you will probably be best in jobs where you have to work with people and need a good background in your field (teacher, repairperson, banker, librarian, doctor, nurse).

1. **Match these words or expressions with their meanings as they are used in the quiz.**

1. quiz	7. in depth	a. need	g. ability
2. select	8. require	b. short test	h. subject
3. at ease	9. keep up with	c. continue to learn about	i. comfortable
4. spare time	10. field	d. choose	j. a lot of experience
5. dislike	11. aptitude	e. as completely as possible	k. free time
6. a good background	12. is designed to	f. is supposed to	l. don't enjoy

2. **Do you have a job now? Are you thinking about a future career or career change? Does the analysis of your score on the quiz help you decide which line of work is ideal for you?**

P R E V I E W

FUNCTIONS/THEMES	LANGUAGE	FORMS
State a condition	Are you going to go camping this weekend? If it stops raining./Not unless it stops raining./Not if it doesn't stop raining.	*If* vs. *unless*
State a prohibition	You're not supposed to park here unless you have a permit. You don't have to eat the hamburgers.	*Be supposed to* vs. *have to* in negative statements
Describe an injury	Did you hurt yourself? Yes. I have this sharp pain between my shoulders, and I think I might have sprained my ankle. I'd better call an ambulance.	
Report requests and instructions	She told me not to come over. He told me to take it easy and not lift anything heavy.	Reported speech with imperatives

Preview the conversations.

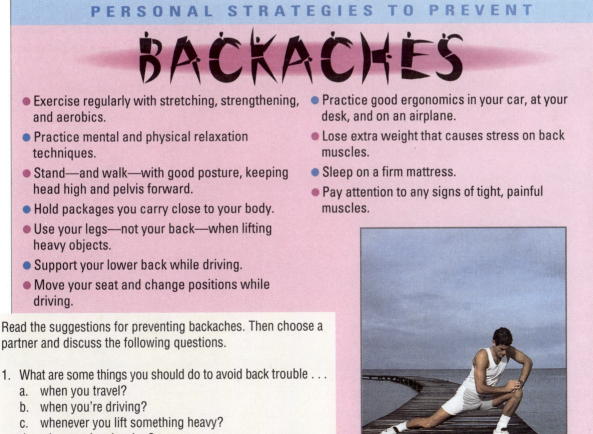

PERSONAL STRATEGIES TO PREVENT

BACKACHES

- Exercise regularly with stretching, strengthening, and aerobics.
- Practice mental and physical relaxation techniques.
- Stand—and walk—with good posture, keeping head high and pelvis forward.
- Hold packages you carry close to your body.
- Use your legs—not your back—when lifting heavy objects.
- Support your lower back while driving.
- Move your seat and change positions while driving.

- Practice good ergonomics in your car, at your desk, and on an airplane.
- Lose extra weight that causes stress on back muscles.
- Sleep on a firm mattress.
- Pay attention to any signs of tight, painful muscles.

Read the suggestions for preventing backaches. Then choose a partner and discuss the following questions.

1. What are some things you should do to avoid back trouble . . .
   a. when you travel?
   b. when you're driving?
   c. whenever you lift something heavy?
   d. when you're sleeping?
2. Do you have any other tips for preventing back pain?
3. Have you (or has anyone you know) ever had a health problem or an injury which limited your (his or her) activity?

56. Are you O.K.?

Dr. Helen Lozano is a resident in internal medicine at Sunrise Hospital. It's Saturday morning, and she's having breakfast with her husband, Victor, and their children, Rick and Anna.

A

Helen You know, this is the first Saturday I've had off in months.

Victor You mean you don't have to go to the hospital at all?

Helen That's right. I asked them not to call me unless it's absolutely necessary.

Victor Well, what are you planning to do with all this free time?

Helen Maybe I'll clean out the attic.

Victor Well, remember, you're not supposed to lift anything heavy.

Helen Now who's the doctor, you or me?

Victor I just don't want you to have any more back trouble. Your doctor said to take it easy.

Helen Oh, Victor. Don't nag!

Victor O.K., O.K. . . . Hey, don't forget . . . we're invited to the Grays' for dinner tonight.

Helen What time are we supposed to be there?

Victor At about seven.

Helen Should I make dessert?

Victor Not unless you want to. They said not to go to any trouble.

Rick What about me? Do I have to go, too?

Helen Not if you don't want to. But I know they'd love to see you.

Rick Hey, what's that you're drawing?

Anna You're not supposed to look until it's finished.

B

Helen You won't believe how much stuff I'm getting rid of . . . .

Victor WATCH OUT! (*Helen slips on a toy and falls down the stairs.*) Helen, are you O.K.? Did you hurt yourself?

Helen Yes. I have this sharp pain between my shoulders, and I think I might have sprained my ankle.

Victor (*To Anna*) How many times have I told you not to leave your toys around? (*Anna starts to cry.*)

Helen You'd better call an ambulance, Victor. I guess I'm going to the hospital after all.

Figure it out

1. Listen to the conversations and check (√) the statements that are implied.

1. _√_ Helen usually works on Saturdays.
2. ____ Frank is a doctor, too.
3. ____ Helen has had some back trouble in the past.
4. ____ Helen didn't know about the invitation to the Grays' for dinner.
5. ____ Helen doesn't want to make dessert to take to the Grays'.
6. ____ Anna had left a toy on the stairs where Helen slipped.
7. ____ Helen thinks she has some serious injuries.
8. ____ Helen decides to go to work after all.

2. Choose *a* or *b* to complete each conversation.

1. Why are you getting rid of that?
   a. Because I don't need it.
   b. Because I need it.

2. Do you have the day off?
   a. No, I don't have to work at all.
   b. No, I have to work after all.

3. Is it O.K. to park my car here?
   a. No, you're not supposed to.
   b. No, you don't have to.

4. Are you going to go to work?
   a. Not if I have to.
   b. Not unless I have to.

5. What time are we supposed to meet the Grays?
   a. They said to meet them at seven.
   b. They said not to go to any trouble.

3. Find the sentences that mean the opposite of the following sentences.

1. You mean you have to go to the hospital today?
   You mean you don't have to go to the hospital at all?
2. They said to go to a lot of trouble.
3. I asked them to call me for any reason at all.
4. But remember, you're supposed to lift heavy things.
5. Not if you want to. (two answers)

57. Not unless it stops raining.

1 ▶ **Listen to the three possible conversations and practice them with a partner.**
▶ **Act out similar conversations, using the information in the boxes.**

A Are you going to go camping this weekend?

B Yes, if it stops raining. **B** Not unless it stops raining. **B** Not if it doesn't stop raining.

Are you going to . . .
go camping this weekend?
take another English course?
work on Saturday?
watch TV tonight?

Some conditions	
Yes, if Not unless	there's something good on. it stops raining. I do well in this one. I have to.

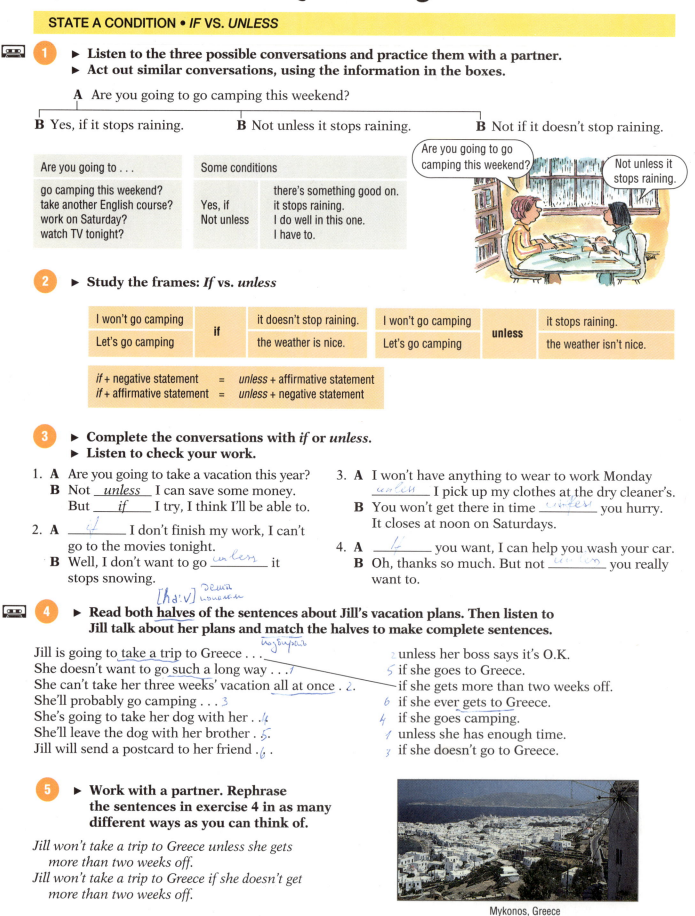

Are you going to go camping this weekend?

Not unless it stops raining.

2 ▶ **Study the frames: *If* vs. *unless***

I won't go camping		it doesn't stop raining.
Let's go camping	**if**	the weather is nice.

I won't go camping		it stops raining.
Let's go camping	**unless**	the weather isn't nice.

if + negative statement	=	*unless* + affirmative statement
if + affirmative statement	=	*unless* + negative statement

3 ▶ **Complete the conversations with *if* or *unless*.**
▶ **Listen to check your work.**

1. **A** Are you going to take a vacation this year?
   B Not _unless_ I can save some money.
   But _____if_____ I try, I think I'll able to.

2. **A** _____if_____ I don't finish my work, I can't go to the movies tonight.
   B Well, I don't want to go _unless_ it stops snowing.

3. **A** I won't have anything to wear to work Monday _unless_ I pick up my clothes at the dry cleaner's.
   B You won't get there in time _unless_ you hurry. It closes at noon on Saturdays.

4. **A** _____if_____ you want, I can help you wash your car.
   B Oh, thanks so much. But not _unless_ you really want to.

4 ▶ **Read both halves of the sentences about Jill's vacation plans. Then listen to Jill talk about her plans and match the halves to make complete sentences.**

Jill is going to take a trip to Greece . . .	2 unless her boss says it's O.K.
She doesn't want to go such a long way . . . 1	5 if she goes to Greece.
She can't take her three weeks' vacation all at once . 2.	if she gets more than two weeks off.
She'll probably go camping . . . 3	6 if she ever gets to Greece.
She's going to take her dog with her . .4	4 if she goes camping.
She'll leave the dog with her brother . 5.	1 unless she has enough time.
Jill will send a postcard to her friend .6 .	3 if she doesn't go to Greece.

5 ▶ **Work with a partner. Rephrase the sentences in exercise 4 in as many different ways as you can think of.**

Jill won't take a trip to Greece unless she gets more than two weeks off.
Jill won't take a trip to Greece if she doesn't get more than two weeks off.

Mykonos, Greece

6 ▶ **Listen to the conversation and practice it with a partner.**
▶ **Act out similar conversations, using the information in the box and the pictures below.**

Is it O.K. to . . .

park here?   use this restroom?
exit here?   wash this sweater?

A Is it O.K. to park here?
B You're not supposed to park here unless you have a permit.

unless it's emergency

7 ▶ **Listen to the conversation and practice it with a partner.**
▶ **Act out similar conversations, using the information in the boxes.**

A We're having hamburgers for dinner.
B Oh, no! Not hamburgers again!
A You don't have to eat them if you don't want to.

Some situations
We're having hamburgers for dinner.
We're having fried chicken for dinner. *(x)*
We're invited to a party at the Browns' on Saturday.
I'm going to watch an old Dracula movie on TV.
I'm going to make a pot of herbal tea.

Some objections
You had hamburgers for lunch.
You don't like chicken.
You can't stand the Browns.
Horror movies keep you awake at night.
You think herbal tea tastes awful.

8 ▶ **Study the frame: *Be supposed to* vs. *have to* in negative statements**

(3 + a) прилагательное

You	**'re not supposed to**	have spicy foods.	▶	There's a prohibition.
You	**don't have to**	eat the hamburgers.	▶	There's no obligation.

(hafta)

The negative form of *be supposed to* means that something isn't permitted.
  You*'re not supposed to* have spicy foods. (Your doctor told you not to.)
The negative form of *have to* means that something isn't necessary or required.
  You *don't have to* eat the hamburgers. (Eat them only if you want to.)

9 ▶ **Complete each conversation with a negative form of *be supposed to* or *have to.***
▶ **Listen to check your work.**

1. **A** Remember, you *'re not supposed to* eat spicy foods.
   B You *don't have to* tell me. I know.

2. **A** Come to the picnic. There'll be hamburgers . . .
   B But I'm a vegetarian.
   A Well, you *don't have to* eat the hamburgers. There'll be lots of other things—like chocolate cake!
   B I *'m not supposed to* eat chocolate. I'm allergic to it.

3. **A** Karen is willing to drive to the picnic, but she *isn't supposed to* drive at night. She can't see very well when it's dark.
   B She *doesn't have to* drive at night. If the picnic *will* ends late, one of us can drive back.

4. **A** Do I need a library card to use the library?
   B You *don't have / 're supposed to (?)* have one to use the library—only to take books out. But you'll have to drink your coffee outside. You *'re not supposed to* bring food or drinks into the library.

10 ▶ **Talk to your classmates. Make a list of things you're not supposed to do in your English class and things you don't have to do.**

We're not supposed to talk during a test.
We don't have to use the language lab unless we want to.

58. Did you hurt yourself?

1 ▶ What happened to each person? Match the pictures with the sentences.
   ▶ Listen to check your work.

4 a. While I was chopping up some vegetables, I cut my finger.

6 b. I accidentally bumped into the door and hurt my elbow.

3 c. I was roller blading when I lost my balance. I fell and bruised my knee.

example

2 d. I tripped on a banana peel. I fell and sprained my ankle.

1 e. I was lifting something. I guess I did it the wrong way. Now I have this pain in my lower back.

5 f. I was skiing when I fell down and broke my leg.

2 ▶ Listen to the two possible conversations and practice them with a partner.
   ▶ Imagine you've had some injuries. Act out similar conversations, using the information below.

A Did you hurt yourself?

B Yes. I have this sharp pain between my shoulders, and I think I sprained my ankle.

B No, I think I'm O.K.

A I'd better call an ambulance.

Some problems and injuries
I have this sharp pain between my shoulders.
I have this dull pain in my lower back.
I think I sprained my ankle.
I think I broke my arm.
I cut my finger. / I bruised my knee.
I hurt my elbow. / I pulled a muscle.

Some ways to describe pain		
I have this	sharp ⊃	pain . . .
	dull —	
	nagging	
	chronic K	
	severe (ə.íʰ)	
	on-again-off-again	

Some responses
I'd better call an ambulance.
I'd better call a doctor.
You'd better not move.
I'll put on a bandage.
You'd better wash it with soap.
You'd better put some ice on it.

3 ▶ Work with a partner. Have you ever had an injury? Describe the injury and tell your partner how it happened. Then tell the class about your partner's injury.

Omar broke his arm a long time ago. He was riding a horse, and he fell off.
Nancy once burned her hand. She was cooking when she spilled boiling water on it.

59. What did the doctor tell you?

1 ▶ **Study the frames: Reported speech with imperatives**

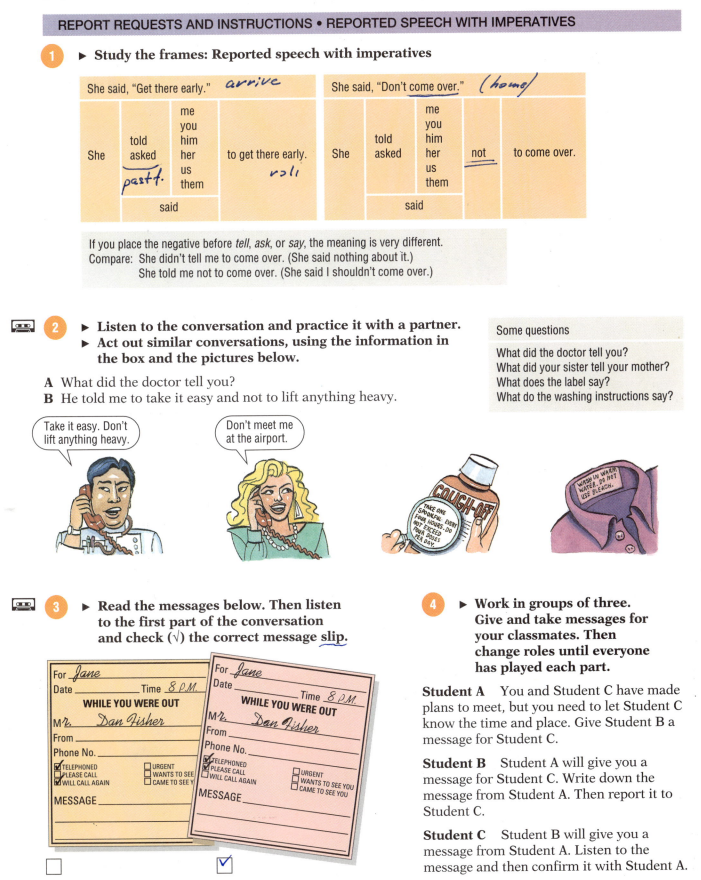

She said, "Get there early." *arrive*

She	told asked *past t.* said	me you him her us them	to get there early. *v>li*

She said, "Don't come over." *(home)*

She	told asked said	me you him her us them	not	to come over.

If you place the negative before *tell*, *ask*, or *say*, the meaning is very different.
Compare: She didn't tell me to come over. (She said nothing about it.)
She told me not to come over. (She said I shouldn't come over.)

2 ▶ **Listen to the conversation and practice it with a partner.**
▶ **Act out similar conversations, using the information in the box and the pictures below.**

Some questions

What did the doctor tell you?
What did your sister tell your mother?
What does the label say?
What do the washing instructions say?

A What did the doctor tell you?
B He told me to take it easy and not to lift anything heavy.

Take it easy. Don't lift anything heavy.

Don't meet me at the airport.

COUGH-OFF TAKE ONE SPOONFUL EVERY FOUR HOURS. DO NOT EXCEED FOUR DOSES PER DAY.

WASH IN WARM WATER. DO NOT USE BLEACH.

3 ▶ **Read the messages below. Then listen to the first part of the conversation and check (√) the correct message slip.**

For *Jane*	
Date _____	Time *8 P.M.*
WHILE YOU WERE OUT	
Mr. *Dan Fisher*	
From _____	
Phone No. _____	
☑ TELEPHONED	☐ URGENT
☐ PLEASE CALL	☐ WANTS TO SEE Y
☑ WILL CALL AGAIN	☐ CAME TO SEE Y
MESSAGE _____	

For *Jane*	
Date _____	Time *8 P.M.*
WHILE YOU WERE OUT	
Mr. *Dan Fisher*	
From _____	
Phone No. _____	
☑ TELEPHONED	☐ URGENT
☐ PLEASE CALL	☐ WANTS TO SEE YOU
☐ WILL CALL AGAIN	☐ CAME TO SEE YOU
MESSAGE _____	

☐   ☑

▶ **Listen to the rest of the conversation and complete the message.**

4 ▶ **Work in groups of three. Give and take messages for your classmates. Then change roles until everyone has played each part.**

Student A You and Student C have made plans to meet, but you need to let Student C know the time and place. Give Student B a message for Student C.

Student B Student A will give you a message for Student C. Write down the message from Student A. Then report it to Student C.

Student C Student B will give you a message from Student A. Listen to the message and then confirm it with Student A.

60. I had to go somewhere at three.

Lou has arrived at the Riveras' house early to talk about a problem they're having.

1

Anita	I hope Kate's O.K.
Lou	Oh, she is. She just had to take care of something. She'll be back to work on Monday. In fact, we should be able to finish your place early next week.
Anita	Well, we've been happy with both of you, and Dr. Kim is delighted with the work you've done for her.
Ed	But to get to the reason we wanted to talk to you both . . .
Lou	Yes, I've been wondering what it could be.
Ed	Do you remember that mask we were showing you last week?
Lou	Yes, of course.
Ed	Well, it's missing.
Lou	What?!
Anita	I'm sure I left it on this table, but when I went to set the table last night, the mask was gone. I've turned the house upside down looking for it.
Ed	We thought that either you or Kate might have moved it, maybe to get it out of your way.
Lou	Well, I didn't. Kate might have after I left, but that doesn't make sense if it wasn't in the kitchen.
Anita	Oh, so you left before she did?
Lou	Yes. I had to go somewhere at three, and she stayed behind to finish up some work.
Anita	Well, she couldn't have stayed long. I got here at three thirty, and she was already gone.

2. Figure it out

Say *True*, *False*, or *It doesn't say.*

1. Lou and Kate are also working for Dr. Kim.
2. Anita and Ed are worried because they can't find their mask.
3. Anita hasn't looked for the mask yet.
4. Anita thinks Kate took the mask.
5. Kate left the Riveras' apartment less than a half hour after Lou.

3. Listen in

The Riveras' conversation with Lou is interrupted briefly by a telephone call. Read the statements below. Then listen to the conversations and say *True* or *False.*

1. Lisa is Ed and Anita's niece.
2. Lisa is in the hospital because she broke her arm.
3. Ed's sister doesn't live in the same neighborhood as Ed and Anita.
4. Anita asks Lou not to leave the apartment until she gets back.

61. Your turn

These pictures show dangerous situations. In groups, discuss why they are dangerous. Here are some words you may want to use: *wheel* (n), *plug* (n, v), *белка* *(electrical) outlet*, *extension cord*, *pot*, *handle* (n), *stove*, *burner*, *lean* (v), *trip* (v).

How to say it

Practice the phrases. Then practice the conversation.

supposed to [səpówstə]   have to [hǽftə]

A You'll have to leave your dog outside, sir. You're not supposed to bring dogs into the store.

B Oh, O.K. I'll have to come back later, then. I can't leave him alone.

62.

HOW SAFE IS YOUR HOME?

Where do you think the greatest number of accidents take place: at work, at home, or on highways? What are the leading causes of injuries?

Do you feel that your home is a safe place and that danger lies only in the outside world? Would you be surprised to learn that your "safe place" could be a very dangerous place? The truth is that accidents at home result in more injuries than motor vehicle and workplace accidents put together. Serious injuries and even death can be caused by accidental falls, fires, burns, poisonings, and electrical hazards.

Falls are the number one cause of accidental deaths in the home every year and the main reason for accidental deaths of the elderly. They are mostly due to slippery surfaces or loose rugs. Fires, often caused by cigarette smoking, are more dangerous for the smoke and poisonous gases they create than for the actual flames. Electrical hazards, responsible for many home fires, are frequently caused by overloaded wires and fixtures. Burns happen most often to children and the elderly, usually in the bathroom, when the water is too hot. The leading cause of accidental deaths at home for people between the ages of 14 and 44 is poisoning, often the result of the misuse of medicines.

Accidents and injuries in the home don't have to happen. They can be prevented if simple precautions are taken.

SAFETY TIPS

IN THE KITCHEN

- Turn all pot handles toward the back of the stove.
- Use a steady step stool when reaching for items on high shelves.
- Keep a fire extinguisher nearby.
- Keep knives and sharp objects in a safe place.
- Store cleaning materials and poisons in their original containers and lock them away if you have small children.

IN THE BATHROOM

- Set the hot water heater at a temperature less than 120 degrees F (48.9 degrees C).
- Don't use electrical appliances like radios and hair dryers near water, and never touch them with wet hands.
- Keep medicines and vitamins clearly labeled and store them in childproof containers.

THROUGHOUT THE HOUSE

- Don't plug too many appliances into the same wall outlet or extension cord.
- Make sure rugs and carpets are secure. Never hide an electrical cord under a rug.
- If an electrical cord is damaged in any way, do not use it. Have it repaired or replaced.
- Keep hallways and stairs well lighted and free from clutter.
- Install smoke detectors and keep them in working order.
- If you smoke, never smoke in bed and be careful not to smoke in a place where you might fall asleep.
- Keep emergency numbers next to the telephone.

Read the article and answer these questions.

1. Name at least two ways you can prevent fires at home. What other precautions can you take to minimize damage in case there is a fire in your home?

2. Name at least three ways you can take safety precautions with electrical appliances.

3. What are some home safety precautions you can take *especially* if you have small children?

4. What are some of the greatest risks for the elderly at home?

5. What kinds of emergency numbers should you keep near the telephone?

PREVIEW

FUNCTIONS/THEMES	LANGUAGE	FORMS
Talk about problems Give advice Show concern	I haven't been getting much sleep lately. If I were you, I'd take some time off. Have you been getting enough exercise?	The present perfect continuous
Talk about moods and feelings	I'm in a really bad mood. I feel like quitting my job. I know how that is. I've felt like that myself.	
Give warnings and advice	You'd better not push yourself too hard, or you'll be exhausted.	*Had better* and *had better not* Reflexive pronouns
Say thank you	Thanks for the advice. Don't mention it.	

Preview the conversations.

Ask Doctor Malcolm

It is said that today we have more stress in our lives than ever before. We live at a faster pace, and as a result, we sometimes feel exhausted, pressured, tense, depressed, and anxious. Take this person, for example, whose letter I just received. (F)

Dear Dr. Malcolm:

I've been under tremendous pressure lately. I've been working twelve hours a day to get a very important job done. I'm always tired, and I've been in a bad mood for weeks. I get angry over the most unimportant things. I used to swim for exercise, but I haven't been to a pool in months. There never seems to be any time. In fact, there doesn't seem to be any time for anything—not even for just enjoying myself with friends once in a while. What can I do?

—CAN'T GO ON LIKE THIS

Read Dr. Malcolm's column. Then, as a class, discuss CAN'T GO ON's problem. What advice should Dr. Malcolm give to this person?

63. If I were you . . .

Jennifer, Fred, and Sara are employees at a publishing company. Jennifer and Fred, are having their morning coffee when they are interrupted by their boss, Howard Thompson.

A

Mr. Thompson What do you think this is, a social hour? Maybe if you two did less talking, you'd get more work done. (*Slams* his office door)

B

Sara Don't take it personally. Mr. Thompson hasn't been himself lately.
Fred That's for sure.
Jennifer He's been in a bad mood for weeks.

Sara Howard, maybe it's none of my business, but . . . well, you haven't been yourself lately. I mean, you've been losing your temper over nothing. . . .

Howard I know. I shouldn't have blown up like that. I don't know what came over me. And it's not just here. I've been getting into arguments with Linda and yelling at the kids. . . .

Sara Have you been doing anything besides working?

Howard Not really. I haven't been getting much sleep either. But what can I do? I've got to get this work done.

Sara Well, you'd better not push yourself too hard, or you'll get sick. Then you won't be able to get *anything* done.

Howard I'm under so much pressure, Sara. Sometimes I just feel like quitting.

Sara I know how that is, Howard. I've felt like that myself. Listen, if I were you, I'd take some time off and get away for a while. You can't go on at this pace.

Howard You're right. Thanks for listening, Sara. And thanks for the good advice.

Sara And I'd cut down on the coffee too. It makes you even more nervous. . . .

Howard O.K., O.K. That's enough advice! (*Laughs*)

Figure it out

1. Listen to the conversations and choose *a* or *b*.

1. Howard yells at Fred and Jennifer
   a. because their work is poor.
   b. for no real reason.

2. Linda is probably
   a. Howard's wife.
   b. Howard's secretary.

3. Howard is under a lot of pressure
   a. at home.
   b. at work.

4. Sara thinks Howard should
   a. take some time off.
   b. find a new job.

5. Sara thinks Howard's problems come from
   a. too much coffee.
   b. overwork.

2. Find another way to say it.

1. I have to finish this work.
2. I don't know the reason I behaved that way.
3. I've been arguing with Linda and screaming at my children.
4. You've been getting angry for no reason.
5. Sometimes I just want to quit.
6. You should drink less coffee too.
7. Don't think that you did anything wrong.
8. Maybe I shouldn't give my opinion.

64. If I were you, I'd take some time off.

1 ► Listen to the conversation and practice it with a partner.
► Act out similar conversations, using the information in the boxes.

A I haven't been getting much sleep lately.
B If I were you, I'd take some time off.

If I were you, I'd take some time off.

Some problems	Some advice
I haven't been getting much sleep.	Go see a doctor.
I've been working day and night.	Take some time off.
I've been feeling so nervous.	Try to slow down a little.
My knee has been hurting me.	Drink less coffee.

2 ► Listen to the conversation. What advice does Maria's friend give her?

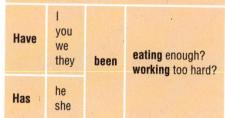

3 ► Study the frames: The present perfect continuous

Information questions

Why	have	I you we they	been	feeling tired?
	has	he she		

Affirmative and negative statements

I You We They	've haven't	been	working hard. sleeping enough.
He She	's hasn't		

Yes-no questions

Have	I you we they	been	eating enough? working too hard?
Has	he she		

Short answers

Yes,	I you we they	have.
No,		haven't.
Yes,	he she	has.
No,		hasn't.

Notice how negative questions are formed in the present perfect continuous.
Hasn't he *been working* too hard?
Why *haven't* you *been taking* any time off?

Notice how tag questions are formed in the present perfect continuous.
She's been working very hard, *hasn't she*?
You haven't been sleeping well, *have you*?

4 ▶ Complete each conversation with a sentence from the box.
▶ Listen to check your work.
▶ Practice the conversations with a partner.

> No, I haven't. I've been coughing and sneezing for two weeks.
> Have you been getting enough exercise?
> I know. I haven't been getting enough sleep.
> You've been losing your temper a lot lately.

1. **A** _Have you been getting enough exercise?_
   B I guess not. I really should take up a sport.

A _You've been losing your temper a lot lately_
   B Yeah. I'm just in a bad mood all the time.

3. **A** You look awfully tired.
   B _I know. I haven't been getting enough sleep last night_

4. **A** You still haven't gotten rid of that cold, have you?
   B _No, I haven't. I've been coughing & sneezing for two weeks._

5 ▶ All day long, patients come into Dr. Barrett's office and talk about their problems. Complete the conversations, using a form of the present perfect continuous and the verbs in parentheses.
▶ Listen to check your work.

1. **A** So, Mrs. Park, how _have you been feeling_ (feel) lately?
   B I _'ve been_ (feel) really tired, and I _haven't been_ (not/concentrate) very well at work.
   A _Did you_ (sleep) well at night? *[Have you been]*
   B No. I _'ve had been_ (have) trouble falling asleep, and I _woke up_ (wake up) in the middle of the night. *[have been]*

2. **A** I _'ve been getting_ (get) terrible headaches, and my hands _'ve been_ (shake) a lot.
   B _Do you_ (drink) more coffee than usual? *[Have been]*
   A No, I don't think I _'ve been have_ *[you have]*

3. **A** Mr. Burns, you _haven't_ (go off) your diet again, _have you_? Why _have you been_ (not/follow) it? *[been going off]*
   B Well, I _'ve been_ (feel) very tense lately, and when I'm tense, I eat.

4. **A** How long _have been_ (cough) like that? *[you] [anything]*
   B For about a month.
   A _Has you be_ (get) worse? *[(o)]*
   B Yes, I'm afraid it _been getting worse._ / _it has._
   A You _'ve not been_ (not/take) very good care of yourself, _have you_ ?
   B No, I guess I _haven't_ .

6 ▶ Work in groups. Read the letter to "Dear Steve," an advice column in a newspaper. Discuss the problem and decide what advice you would give.

> ## Dear Steve,
>
> I'm 25 years old and recently married. Both my husband and I have full-time jobs. Since we got married, I've been doing all of the cooking and most of the household chores. Lately he's been getting home from work in the evening a half hour earlier than me, but he just waits for me to get home and fix his dinner. I don't think that's fair. I've been thinking about talking it over with him, but I don't want to start an argument.
>
> —NEWLYWED

▶ Read Steve's answer on page 165. Do you agree with his advice? (There are no "correct answers.")

Unit 10 **105**

65. Sometimes I feel like quitting.

TALK ABOUT MOODS AND FEELINGS

1 ▶ Listen to the five conversations. Is the first speaker in each conversation in a good mood or a bad mood? Check (√) the correct box.

	Good mood	Bad mood
1.	√	
2.		√
3.	√	√
4.		√
5.	√	

A good mood

A bad mood

2 ▶ Listen to the three possible conversations and practice them with a partner.
▶ Act out similar conversations, using the information in the box. Imagine first that you are in a good mood, then a bad mood.

A I'm in a really good mood.
I feel like going dancing.

B I'm in a really good mood myself.

B Really? I don't feel like doing anything.

A I'm in a really bad mood. I feel like quitting my job.
B I know how that is. I've felt like that myself.

I feel like . . .	
going dancing.	quitting my job.
going out tonight.	making a big change in my life.
having a good time.	crying.
doing something exciting.	yelling at everyone.

3 ▶ Read the survey below. Then ask five classmates if they're ever moody. Find out what they feel like doing when they're in a good mood or a bad mood. Report to the class.

Are you ever moody?

Hae Sook Choi, 24
I guess I am, but I don't always show my true feelings. I mean, sometimes at work I feel like screaming, yet I always try to put on a happy face. But when I'm in a really good mood, and I feel like singing, I try to stay under control too.

Adam Green, 16
Yes! Sometimes I feel great; other times I feel like crying. And my moods change really fast too. My dad says it's all part of being a teenager.

13 – 19

4 ▶ **Listen to the conversation and practice it with a partner.**
▶ **Act out similar conversations, using the information below or your own ideas.**

A I've been working sixty hours a week.
B You'd better not push yourself too hard, or you'll be exhausted.
A You're probably right.

Some problems

I've been working sixty hours a week.
I've only been eating one meal a day.
This is my fourth cup of coffee this evening.
I'm not sure how to use this electric knife.

If you. . .	you'll . . .
push yourself too hard,	be exhausted.
don't take care of yourself,	get sick.
drink any more coffee,	have trouble sleeping.
aren't careful,	hurt yourself.

5 ▶ **Study the frame: Reflexive pronouns**

I hurt **myself**. You cut **yourself**.	▶ as direct objects
He bought **himself** a new car. She built a table for **herself**.	▶ as indirect objects
We should take care of **ourselves**. You only think of **yourselves**.	▶ as objects of prepositions
They've felt like that **themselves**.	▶ for emphasis
He hasn't been **himself** lately. We really enjoyed **ourselves**.	▶ in idioms

Reflexive pronouns may follow the preposition
by to mean "alone" or "without any help."
  I figured it out *by myself.*

6 ▶ **Complete the letter with reflexive pronouns.**

7 ▶ **Listen to Part 1 of "No Problem," a radio call-in talk show with Dr. Rita. Work with your classmates. What advice do you think Dr. Rita will give? Discuss your answers and then listen to Dr. Rita's advice in Part 2.**

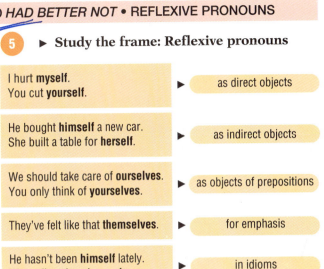

Dear Mom and Dad,
    As usual, I haven't left ____myself____ enough time, so this will just be a short note. The big news is that we bought _ourselves_ skis and have taken up skiing. The children love it, but I sometimes worry that they might hurt _themselves_. They're not as careful as Pat and I are.
    Pat's hard at work studying for her law exams. She's pushing _herself_ very hard, maybe too hard, but you know Pat. I hope you're feeling better, Dad. Make sure that he takes care of _himself_, Mom. We hope you enjoy _yourselves_ on your vacation in Hawaii. I'll write again real soon.
                              Love,
                              Roger

8 ▶ **Listen to the conversation and practice it with a partner.**
▶ **Act out similar conversations, using the pictures below and the information in the box.**

A Thanks for the advice.
B Oh, don't mention it.

Some ways to respond to "Thank you"

Don't mention it. My pleasure. No problem.	You're welcome. You're more than welcome.

If I were you . . .

Thanks for the advice.

Thanks for having us over.

Thanks for helping with the dishes.

66. What do you mean?

It's Saturday afternoon, and Lou is spending some time with his friends John and Carol Thomas.

1

John Don't you think you've been pushing yourself too hard, Lou? You don't seem your usual relaxed self.

Lou Well, I have a lot on my mind.

Carol What's the matter?

Lou There've been some pretty strange things going on, and I've been closing my eyes to them up to now. But lately, it's been getting harder and harder not to put two and two together.

John What do you mean?

Lou It has to do with Kate. I told you, didn't I, that she didn't come to work yesterday?

John Yes, and she didn't really explain why.

Lou Well, a valuable African mask was taken from the Riveras' home Thursday afternoon when Kate was alone in the apartment.

Carol You don't think Kate took it, do you?

Lou I've tried not to think so. She seemed like an honest person, but frankly, I'd be surprised if I ever saw her again. Tell me, what do you know about the "dancer crimes"?

2. Figure it out

Check (√) the statements that are implied in the conversation.

1. ✓ John thinks that Lou is a little tense today.
2. ✓ Lou is starting to think that Kate might be involved in the "dancer crimes."
3. ___ Lou is sure that Kate stole the mask.
4. ___ Carol is surprised that Lou suspects Kate.
5. ___ Lou has always thought that Kate might be dishonest.
6. ✓ Lou thinks Kate probably won't return to work.

3. Listen in

Two women in a car nearby are having a conversation. Read the questions below. Then listen to the conversation and answer the questions.

1. What advice does the passenger give to the woman who is driving?
2. Where are the women going?
3. Does the driver take the advice?

67. Your turn

Take a few minutes to fill out the test on stress. Then discuss these questions in groups.

1. How vulnerable are you to stress? If your score on the test shows that you are experiencing a lot of stress, what can you do to reduce the stress in your life?

2. Which items in the test do you think are most important for a healthy life that is low in stress? Which are least important?

3. What advice can you give to a friend or relative who is under a lot of stress at work? At home? At school?

4. Does English study cause you stress? In what ways? What do you think you can do to reduce some of that stress?

How to say it

Practice the conversation.

A I'm in a really good mood today.

B I'm in a good mood myself.

A Really? Why?

B I just bought myself a new car.

How Vulnerable Are You to STRESS?

Take the stress test. Check (✓) each statement that is true for you.

_____ 1. I can usually express my feelings openly at home, work, or school.

✓ 2. I have close friends or family members I can confide in.

_____ 3. I can manage my time effectively and don't feel overwhelmed by work.

✓ 4. In general, I enjoy the work that I do (at work, school, or both).

✓ 5. Overall, I feel that I am doing a good job (at work, school, or both).

_____ 6. Most of the time I feel that someone appreciates the work that I do (my boss, teachers, family members, etc.).

✓ 7. I usually don't worry about unimportant things or things I can't change.

✓ 8. I'm in good health.

✓ 9. I usually get enough sleep at night.

_____ 10. I generally eat a balanced diet.

✓ 11. I get at least half an hour of moderate exercise almost every day.

✓ 12. I usually drink no more than two cups of coffee (or other caffeinated beverages) a day.

✓ 13. I don't smoke.

✓ 14. I take vacations regularly.

_____ 15. I take some quiet time by myself almost every day.

✓ 16. I have hobbies or social activities that I enjoy doing regularly.

_____ 17. I don't worry about money very much.

_____ 18. I don't live or work in a big city.

✓ 19. I usually spend less than half an hour commuting (in each direction) to work or school. *travel*

_____ 20. I make an effort to change my routine from time to time.

_12_ **Total**

Scoring: *To find your score, count the number of statements you checked. If your score is 16–20, you are probably experiencing low to normal stress. If your score is 11–15, you are probably experiencing quite a bit of stress. If your score is 10 or lower, you are probably experiencing a lot of stress. (A higher score means lower stress.)*

68.

How To Reduce STRESS and Be Happy on the Job

by Gary Dessler

What do you think are some reasons for stress on the job? What can employees do to reduce stress? Read the article and see if your ideas match any of those in the article.

Q. Have you any quick, simple suggestions for how I can reduce the stress I'm under at work? I'm a manager in a large bank, and between company politics, customers who don't pay back **their** loans, and my heavy workload, I find myself under what seems to be unrelenting stress and pressure at work. The stress is beginning to affect my work and family life, and any suggestions would be appreciated.

A. Suggestions range from "get more sleep" to "use meditation." But in a recent book, *Stress and the Manager*, Dr. Karl Albrecht suggests the following to reduce stress on the job:

- Build rewarding, pleasant, cooperative relationships with as many of your colleagues and employees as you can.
- Don't bite off more than you can chew. Take on only those assignments that you know you have time for.
- Build an especially effective and supportive relationship with your boss. Understand **his or her** problems and help the boss to understand **yours.**
- Negotiate realistic deadlines on important projects with your boss. Be prepared to propose deadlines yourself, rather than have them imposed.
- Study the future. Learn as much as you can about likely coming events, so that you can anticipate **them** well in advance.
- Find time every day for detachment and relaxation.

- Take a walk now and then to keep your body refreshed and alert.
- Make a noise survey of your office area and find ways to reduce unnecessary racket.
- Get away from your office from time to time for a change of scene and a change of mind.
- Reduce the amount of trivia to which you give your attention. Delegate routine paperwork to others whenever possible.
- Limit interruptions. Try to schedule certain periods of "interruptability" each day and save other periods of time for your own purposes.
- Make sure you know how to delegate effectively.
- Don't put off dealing with distasteful problems such as counseling a problem employee.
- Make a constructive "worry list." Write down the problems that concern you and beside **each** write down what you're going to do about **it,** so that none of the problems will continue to bother you unconsciously.

---

1. **Read the article. Then find the highlighted words and say what they refer to. They all refer to something that has already been mentioned.**

1. their	3. yours	5. each
2. his or her	4. them	6. it

2. **Which of the following suggestions does the author make? Say *True* or *False*.**

1. Suggest your own deadlines, rather than waiting for your boss to give them to you.
2. Try not to think about what will happen in the future.
3. Never allow interruptions.
4. Give work to other employees, if possible, rather than doing everything yourself.
5. Don't spend time thinking about problems.
6. Take on as much work as you can, without worrying about how much time it will take.
7. Try to understand your boss's point of view.
8. Postpone taking action on a problem if you know it will upset you.

3. **Do you agree with the suggestions in the article for how to reduce stress? Can you think of some ways to reduce stress in your life, whether you are working or not?**

PREVIEW

FUNCTIONS/THEMES	LANGUAGE	FORMS
Greet someone after a long time	I haven't seen you in ages. I've been meaning to call you, but I've been so busy.	
Catch up on what someone's been doing	What have you been doing lately? I've been playing a lot of tennis. In fact, I've played three nights this week.	The present perfect continuous vs. the present perfect
Discuss possible plans	Do you want to play tennis sometime? Sure. If I have time next week, I'll give you a call.	
Imagine something Express a wish or fantasy	If I had more money, I'd travel around the world. I'd fit into this suit if I lost a few pounds.	Conditional sentences
Give unwanted advice	If you got up earlier, you wouldn't be late.	

Preview the conversations.

Rose! How have you been?

Mike! I haven't seen you in so long!

Imagine you haven't seen your partner in a long time and you've just met by chance.

Student A
Since you last saw Student B, you've gotten a new job. Find out what's new in Student B's life. Suggest that you get together one night next week.

Student B
Since you last saw Student A, you've been taking tennis lessons. Find out what Student A's been doing. You'd like to get together, but you're busy every night next week except Tuesday, and you might have to work late then.

Unit 11 **111**

UNIT 11 • LESSONS 69—74

69. If I had more time . . .

🔊 Rose is looking for some information in the library when she runs into Mike, a friend of hers.

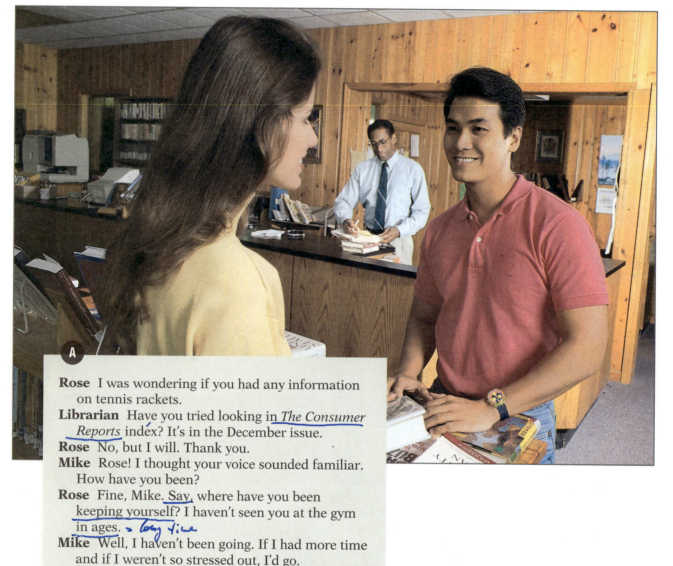

A

Rose I was wondering if you had any information on tennis rackets.
Librarian Have you tried looking in *The Consumer Reports* index? It's in the December issue.
Rose No, but I will. Thank you.
Mike Rose! I thought your voice sounded familiar. How have you been?
Rose Fine, Mike. Say, where have you been keeping yourself? I haven't seen you at the gym in ages. → long time
Mike Well, I haven't been going. If I had more time and if I weren't so stressed out, I'd go.
Rose You *do* look tired.   4 under stress

get yjepung

Figure it out

1. Listen to the conversations and answer the questions with *Mike, Rose,* or *Both.*

1. Who's interested in getting a new tennis racket?
2. Who belongs to a gym?
3. Who hasn't been going to the gym recently?
4. Who's been under a lot of stress recently?
5. Who's been playing a lot of tennis lately?
6. Who's been working on weekends lately?
7. Who would like to get together to play tennis?

2. Find another way to say it.

1. How are you?
2. It's true that you look tired.
3. I haven't had time, and I've been under a lot of pressure. Otherwise, I would go.
4. Why have you been working so hard?
5. I've thought of calling you many times.
6. Let's play tennis together.

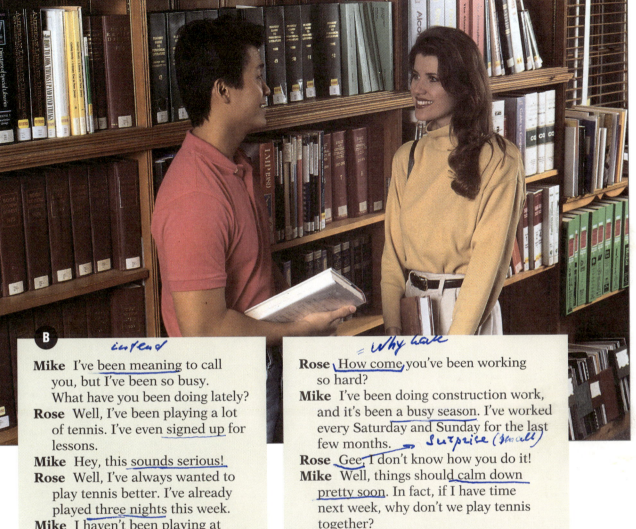

B

intend

Mike I've been meaning to call you, but I've been so busy. What have you been doing lately?

Rose Well, I've been playing a lot of tennis. I've even signed up for lessons.

Mike Hey, this sounds serious!

Rose Well, I've always wanted to play tennis better. I've already played three nights this week.

Mike I haven't been playing at all lately. I've just had too much work.

= Why have

Rose How come you've been working so hard?

Mike I've been doing construction work, and it's been a busy season. I've worked every Saturday and Sunday for the last few months. → *Surprise (small)*

Rose Gee, I don't know how you do it!

Mike Well, things should calm down pretty soon. In fact, if I have time next week, why don't we play tennis together?

Rose Let's do that. Give me a call, and we can set up a time.

---

3. Choose *a* or *b*.

1. How come **b** so hard?
   a. have you been working
   b. you've been working

2. If I ____ time next week, I'll play tennis with you.
   a. had
   b. have

3. **b** tennis three nights this week.
   a. I've been playing
   b. I've played

had. unreal

4. If I **a** time, I'd go to the gym.
   a. had
   b. have   → *I will*

5. I haven't gone to the gym in months because
   b such long hours.
   a. I've worked
   b. I've been working

70. I've been meaning to call you.

1 ► Listen to the conversation and practice it with a partner.
► Act out similar conversations. Imagine you haven't seen your partner for a long time, and you've just run into each other. Use the expressions in the box.

A Rose! I haven't seen you in ages!
B Mike! I've been meaning to call you, but I've been so busy.
A So, how have you been? . . .

I've been meaning to . . .	but . . .
call you, get in touch with you, find out how you've been, invite you over,	I've been so busy. I've had so much work. I haven't had a free minute. I just haven't had a chance.

2 ► Walk around the classroom, greeting your classmates briefly. Imagine you haven't seen them for a long time.

CATCH UP ON WHAT SOMEONE'S BEEN DOING • THE PRESENT PERFECT CONTINUOUS VS. THE PRESENT PERFECT

3 ► Listen to the two possible conversations and practice them with a partner.
► Act out similar conversations, using the information in the box.

A What have you been doing lately?
B I've been playing a lot of tennis.
A Oh, really?
B Yes. In fact, I've played three nights this week.

B I haven't been doing much of anything.

Some activities	
I've been playing I've played	a lot of tennis. three nights this week.
I've been working I've worked	very hard. three weekends this month.
I've been going I've gone	to the movies a lot. four times this week alone.

4 ► Study the frames: The present perfect continuous vs. the present perfect

The present perfect continuous	The present perfect
I've been working very hard.	**I've** always **worked** hard.
I've been trying to find a new job.	**I haven't found** a new job yet.
I've been thinking about where to go on vacation.	**I've** never **gone** to Mexico.
I haven't been feeling well.	**I've worked** every night this week.

Use the present perfect continuous to emphasize that something is ongoing or repetitive.
Use the present perfect with *always*, *yet*, and *never* and when you mention the specific number of times something has happened.

The present perfect continuous refers to something that began in the past and continues into the present. The present perfect often refers to an unspecified time in the past.

  I*'ve been reading* this book. (I haven't finished it.)
  I*'ve read* this book. (I've finished it.)

When a sentence has an adverb or time expression that shows something is ongoing or repetitive, you can often use either the present perfect continuous or the present perfect.

  I*'ve been living* here for four years.
  I*'ve lived* here for four years.

Use the present perfect, not the present perfect continuous, with the verb *be*. In general, use the present perfect with the verbs *seem*, *see*, and *hear*.

  I *haven't been* to the gym lately.
  He*'s seemed* kind of tense recently.

5 ▶ **Listen and match each conversation with the correct picture.**
▶ **Listen again and write what one person in each conversation has been doing lately.**

He's been traveling a lot. _____ _____ _____

6 ▶ **Complete the conversations, using a present perfect or present perfect continuous form of the verbs in parentheses.**

1. **A** I *'ve been trying* (try) to call you all day.
   I *'ve tried* (try) at least five times.
   Where *have you* (be)? *been*
   B I *'ve been* (study) at the library most of the time
   because it *has been* (be) so hot in my apartment.

2. **A** *Have you heard* (hear) from Norma recently?
   B No. She *has not written* (not/write) to me since last summer.
   I guess she *has been* (be) busy with her new job.
   A Yes, I think she *has been* (travel) a lot too.

3. **A** Jill? This is Ed.
   B Oh, hi, Ed.
   A Am I calling too late?
   B No. I *'ve been* (watch) the news on
   TV. I'll just turn it off. . . . So, what
   have you been doing (do) lately?
   A Well, I *'ve been* (practice) my dancing.
   I'm planning to enter a dance contest!
   B Really?

7 ▶ **Ask a classmate what he or she has been doing recently. Keep the conversation going by asking additional questions. Then change roles.**

DISCUSS POSSIBLE PLANS

8 ▶ **Listen to the conversation and practice it with a partner.**
▶ **Act out similar conversations.**

A Do you want to play tennis sometime?
B Sure. If I have time next week, I'll give you a call.

Some plans
Do you want to play tennis sometime? I'm thinking of going shopping on Saturday. Do you want to join me? We'll have to go biking some Sunday. How about going out for dinner one day next week?

Some responses
Sure. If I have time next week, I'll give you a call. I'd like to. Let's make plans the day before. Let's do that. Give me a call and we can set up a time. That would be nice. I'll check my calendar and let you know.

9 ▶ **Work with a partner. Play these roles.**

Student A You're thinking about doing these things on the weekend:

play golf   go shopping
go to the beach   go to a concert
go to a movie   try a new restaurant

Select two activities and suggest them to Student B. Then switch roles.

Student B Student A will suggest some plans for the weekend. Respond to the suggestions without making firm plans. Then switch roles.

71. If I had more time, I'd go.

1 ▶ **Listen to the two possible conversations and practice them with a partner.**
▶ **Act out similar conversations, using the questions in the box.**

A If I had more money, I'd travel around the world.
B Really? If I had more money, I'd try to save it.

A If I had more money, I wouldn't want to work.
B Really? If I had more money, I'd still want to work.

> What would you do if you . . .
>
> had more money?
> weren't so busy?
> were younger/older?
> were/weren't married?

2 ▶ **Interview two classmates. Find out what they would do if they had unlimited time and money. Report to the class.**

Isabel would get her own villa on the Mediterranean and invite all her friends to visit. Hiro would learn how to fly a jet. Then he'd buy one.

3 ▶ **Study the frames: Conditional sentences**

Possible conditions

	Present tense form	Future	
If	I **have** time,	I**'ll play** tennis.	▶ *If I have time* means "I might have time."
	I **don't have** time,	I **won't go** to the gym.	▶ *If I don't have time* means "I might not have time."

Contrary-to-fact conditions

	Past tense form	Conditional	
If	I **had** time,	I**'d play** tennis.	▶ *If I had time* means "I don't have time."
	I **didn't have** time,	I **wouldn't go** to the gym.	▶ *If I didn't have time* means "I have time."
	I **were** you,	I **wouldn't work** so hard.	▶ *If I were you* means "I'm not you."
	I **weren't** so busy,	I**'d be** home more often.	▶ *If I weren't so busy* means "I'm very busy."

> In contrary-to-fact conditional sentences, *were* or *weren't* is used instead of *was* or *wasn't* with all subjects and subject pronouns.
> If it *were* sunny, we'd go swimming.
> If he *weren't* home, the lights would be off.

> Like *can, should, may, might,* and *must,* the modal auxiliary *would* has the same form for all subjects and is followed by the base form of the verb.
> We*'d take* a vacation if we had more money.
> They *wouldn't be* late if they got up on time.
> If you got up earlier, you *wouldn't be* late for work.

4 ▶ **Complete the conditional sentences in the conversations, using the verbs in parentheses.**
▶ **Listen to check your work.**

1. **A** What are you doing this evening?
   B I'm not sure yet. If there _isn't_ (not/be) anything good on TV, I think I _'ll_ (read) a mystery. Or maybe I _'ll_ (go) to bed early.

2. **A** I'm so stressed out!
   B Maybe it's none of my business, but if I _were_ (be) you, I _'d_ (take) some time off.

3. **A** What time will Elena be home?
   B If I _knew_ (know), I _'d_ (tell) you, but unfortunately, she didn't say.
   A Well, if she _gets_ (get) home before 9:00, please have her call me.

4. **A** I'm afraid your flight has been delayed due to bad weather.
   B Oh no! When will it take off?
   A We don't have any information yet. If it _stops_ (stop) snowing this evening, then your flight _'ll_ (depart) sometime tonight.
   B What are the chances that will happen?
   A It's too early to tell. Why don't you take a seat? I _'ll_ (let) you know if I _hear_ (hear) any news.

5 ▶ Read the advertisements and listen to four people talk about their wishes and fantasies. Match the speaker with the ad.

Lose 10 pounds in one week! Drink Slinky chocolate shakes! What have you got to lose?

Quit smoking forever! Try our special chewing gum and you'll never want to smoke again!

Get rich quick! Invest in our no-risk fund and double your money in no time!

See the future! Madame Olga will tell you what the future holds for you. Satisfaction guaranteed!

Learn to speak perfect English in one month! Churchill Institute of Perfect English.

Speed reading! Learn to read 200 pages an hour and remember everything you've read. Study at home, at your own pace.

▶ Work in groups. Do you wish one of the fantasies in the ads (or another fantasy) were true for you? How would your life be different? Report to the class.

GIVE UNWANTED ADVICE

6 ▶ Listen to the conversation and practice it with a partner.
▶ Imagine your partner is worried about each of the problems below, but you aren't very sympathetic. Respond to each one with a contrary-to-fact conditional sentence. Use the ideas in the box or your own ideas.

A I'm always late for work.
B If you got up earlier, you wouldn't be late.

> **Some opinions**
>
> You should get up earlier.
> You should study more.
> You should call them.
> He shouldn't waste much time.
> You should write to your friends.
> You should try to communicate with them.

I'm always late for work.

My grades this semester are terrible.

My friends never call me.

My son can never seem to get his work done.

I never get any interesting mail.

My parents don't understand me.

72. He's only been driving for a week.

Dr. Kim has just had dinner in a restaurant with her husband and their children, Joe and Julia.

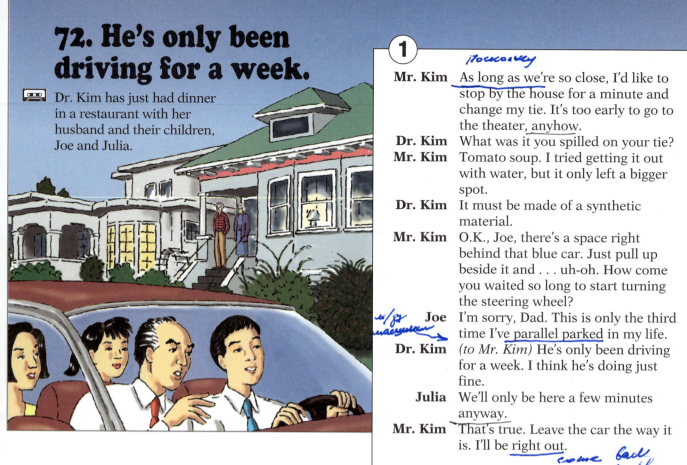

1

Mr. Kim As long as we're so close, I'd like to stop by the house for a minute and change my tie. It's too early to go to the theater, anyhow.

Dr. Kim What was it you spilled on your tie?

Mr. Kim Tomato soup. I tried getting it out with water, but it only left a bigger spot.

Dr. Kim It must be made of a synthetic material.

Mr. Kim O.K., Joe, there's a space right behind that blue car. Just pull up beside it and . . . uh-oh. How come you waited so long to start turning the steering wheel?

Joe I'm sorry, Dad. This is only the third time I've parallel parked in my life.

Dr. Kim *(to Mr. Kim)* He's only been driving for a week. I think he's doing just fine.

Julia We'll only be here a few minutes anyway.

Mr. Kim That's true. Leave the car the way it is. I'll be right out.

2. Listen in

Dr. Kim, Joe, and Julia are listening to the car radio while Mr. Kim is in the house. Read the questions below. Then listen to the radio commercial and answer the questions.

1. Why are the people in the commercial so tired?
2. What suggestion does the commercial make?

3

(Twenty minutes later, Mr. Kim still hasn't returned.)

Julia I thought Dad was just going to change his tie.

Dr. Kim He *has* been in there a long time. I wonder what's keeping him.

4. Figure it out

Choose *a* or *b*.

1. a. The Kims are on their way to dinner.
   b. The Kims are on their way to the theater.

2. a. Mr. Kim wanted to go home to change his tie.
   b. Mr. Kim wanted to go home to wash his tie.

3. a. Mr. Kim got rid of most of the spot with water.
   b. Mr. Kim couldn't get the spot out.

4. a. Joe has just learned how to drive.
   b. Joe doesn't know how to drive.

5. a. Mr. Kim is taking a long time because he's having trouble finding a tie that matches his clothes.
   b. Dr. Kim doesn't know why her husband has been in the house so long.

73. Your turn

**How would you handle these situations? Discuss the problems in groups.
What would you do if . . . ?**

. . . you found an envelope in the street with a lot of cash in it? There is no name or address inside.

. . . your friend asked you if he or she could copy from you during a test?

. . . you found out that a coworker was stealing money from the company? The coworker is a good friend of yours.

. . . you felt someone was punishing his or her child for no reason?

. . . your boss wanted you to fire one of your best workers? You know that your boss wants to give the job to a relative.

. . . you were selling your car and someone offered you a lot more money than it's worth?

How to say it

Practice the conversation.

A What have you been doing lately?
     [əv]   [bn]

B I've been working every weekend.
     [bn]

A Why have you been working so much?
     [əv]   [bn]

B Because I need the money.

74. If I Had A Hammer

Words and Music by
LEE HAYS and PETE SEEGER

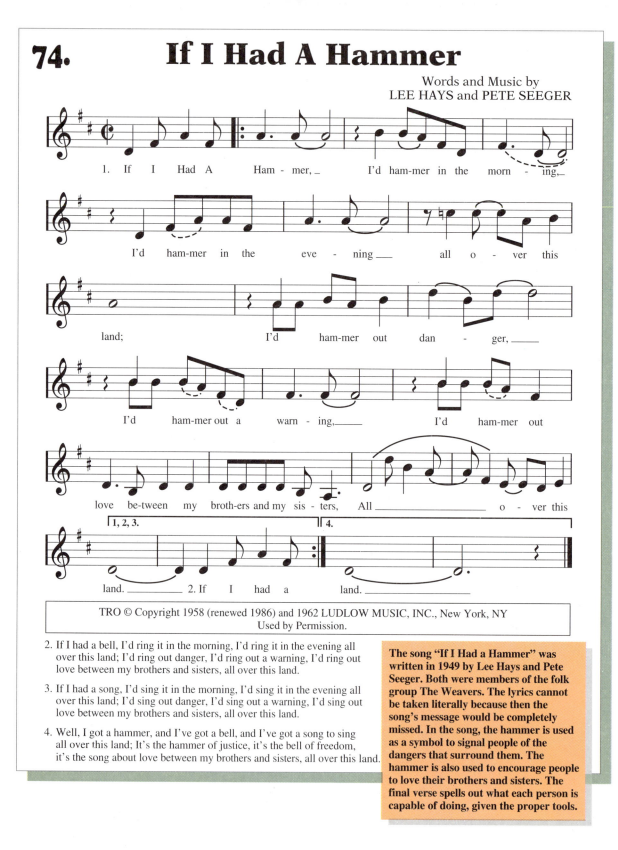

TRO © Copyright 1958 (renewed 1986) and 1962 LUDLOW MUSIC, INC., New York, NY
Used by Permission.

2. If I had a bell, I'd ring it in the morning, I'd ring it in the evening all over this land; I'd ring out danger, I'd ring out a warning, I'd ring out love between my brothers and sisters, all over this land.

3. If I had a song, I'd sing it in the morning, I'd sing it in the evening all over this land; I'd sing out danger, I'd sing out a warning, I'd sing out love between my brothers and sisters, all over this land.

4. Well, I got a hammer, and I've got a bell, and I've got a song to sing all over this land; It's the hammer of justice, it's the bell of freedom, it's the song about love between my brothers and sisters, all over this land.

The song "If I Had a Hammer" was written in 1949 by Lee Hays and Pete Seeger. Both were members of the folk group The Weavers. The lyrics cannot be taken literally because then the song's message would be completely missed. In the song, the hammer is used as a symbol to signal people of the dangers that surround them. The hammer is also used to encourage people to love their brothers and sisters. The final verse spells out what each person is capable of doing, given the proper tools.

Read the words to the song, "If I Had a Hammer," and the paragraph about it. Then discuss these questions.

1. Do you think this is a happy song? A sad song? An optimistic song? Why?
2. The words *hammer* and *bell* are used symbolically: "the hammer of justice" and "the bell of freedom." Can you think of other things that can be used as symbols—for example, a door, a light, a window?
3. What do you think the "message" of this song is? Do you know of other songs with a message?

Review of units 8-11

1 ▶ **Tina is taking a taxi to a movie theater. Complete the conversation between Tina and the driver with an affirmative or a negative form of *be supposed to* or *have to*. Be sure to use the correct tense.**

▶ **Listen to check your work.**

Tina Excuse me, but I think you made a wrong turn. You <u>were supposed to</u> turn left on Wilson.

Driver Oh, didn't you say 200 Winston?

Tina No, 200 *Wilson*. It's O.K., though. You _____ go back. I can walk to the movie theater from here.

Driver Why don't I make a U-turn at the corner?

Tina But you _____ make a U-turn there. There's a sign up ahead.

Driver Well, maybe if I turn left here, I can go back down the next street.

Tina You _____ do that either during rush hour. Really, it's no problem. I _____ wait half an hour for a taxi, so I'm happy I got this close.

Driver Half an hour! I've been driving around all day looking for passengers.

2 ▶ **Tina's friend Frank has been waiting for her in front of the movie theater. Listen to their argument and practice it with a partner.**

Frank I've been waiting here for forty-five minutes! Where have you been?

Tina Sorry. I had to wait a long time to get a taxi.

Frank You were supposed to be here forty minutes ago! And this isn't the first time you've been late.

Tina Look, you don't have to get so upset.

Frank If I were you, I'd be a little more considerate. If you weren't always late, I wouldn't get upset.

Tina Hey, I don't have to listen to this!

Frank Well, you'd better listen, or I won't wait for you again!

▶ **Work with your classmates and answer these questions.**

1. How late is Tina? Why is she late?
2. Has Tina ever been late before? Is Frank sympathetic?
3. If you were Frank, would you be angry?
4. If you were Tina, what would you say or do?

3 ▶ **Imagine you and your partner are roommates. You share an apartment and the household chores. You're going to have an argument similar to the one in exercise 2. Use some or all of the expressions in the box.**

> You were supposed to . . .
> I'm/You're (not) supposed to . . .
> I/You (don't) have to . . .
> You'd better (not) . . . or . . .
> If I were you, I would(n't) . . .
> If I/you . . . I/you would(n't) . . .

Student A Your partner was supposed to take out the garbage this morning and clean the kitchen this afternoon but didn't do either one. It's not the first time this has happened, and you're really annoyed. Tell your partner what you think. You can start like this: *You were supposed to . . .*

Student B You were supposed to take out the garbage this morning and clean the kitchen this afternoon. You had a lot of other things to do today and didn't get around to the household chores. But, you plan to do them tomorrow. Your partner is annoyed with you, but you don't think housework is as important as your partner thinks it is. Respond to what your partner says.

4A

▶ Student A follows the instructions below.
▶ Student B follows the instructions on page 124.

Student A Imagine you and your partner are coworkers, and you're trying to set up a one-hour meeting next week. Here is your calendar at work next week. Take turns suggesting times to meet. If your partner suggests a time when you're busy, say what you have to do at that time. Use infinitives.

Start like this:

A *How about getting together on Monday at 11:00 A.M.?*
B *I'm sorry, but I have a staff meeting to attend at 11:00. What about 10:00? Can you make it then?*
A *No, I can't. I have some urgent letters to write then.*

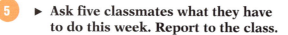

WEEKLY CALENDAR

MONDAY	Call Harris, Martinez, Choi before 10:00 A.M.
	Write to all the sales reps. before 11:00 A.M. (urgent!)
	12 Noon: Lunch appointment with new client
TUESDAY	Write monthly sales report in A.M. (all morning?)
	Read annual report — 500 pages! (all afternoon?)
	Reception for new company president, 4:30 P.M.
WEDNESDAY	Sales conference, all day
THURSDAY	Marketing seminar, 9:00 A.M.–12:30 P.M.
FRIDAY	Flight to Hawaii, 4:00 P.M.

5

▶ Ask five classmates what they have to do this week. Report to the class.

Ricardo has some guests to entertain.
Machiko has a test to study for.

6

▶ Complete the conversation with reflexive pronouns (like *myself*) or object pronouns (like *me*).

Carla I just haven't been <u>myself</u> recently.
Jane What's the matter?
Carla I don't know, but lately I haven't been able to enjoy _____ at all.
Jane You've been working too hard. You really should take better care of _____ .
Carla I know, but there's so much to do. My boss told _____ there was no money for a secretary, so Victor and I have to do everything _____ .
Jane Isn't there even someone to help _____ do the photocopying?
Carla Nobody. And Ray even asked _____ to do some work for him.
Jane Why should you? Can't he do it _____ ?
Carla He decided to take a vacation. Some people think only of _____ .
Jane I know what you mean. Listen, why don't you treat _____ to a nice lunch or buy _____ a present? Maybe you'll feel better.

7

▶ Listen to the conversation.
▶ Act out a similar conversation with a partner. Student A: Make a suggestion using the ideas in the box below or your own ideas. If Student B doesn't agree, continue making more suggestions. Student B: Respond to Student A's suggestions by saying what you feel like doing or don't feel like doing.

Bill Let's go for a walk.
Carla I don't feel like going for a walk.
Bill Then why don't we go to a movie?
Carla I don't feel like seeing a movie either.
Bill Then what do you want to do tonight?
Carla I feel like staying home.

Some suggestions

Let's go for a walk.
Why don't we go to a movie?
How about going camping this weekend?
Do you want to eat out?
Is there anything good on TV?

8 ▶ Ken Plansky is a repairman. One winter afternoon he gets a call from a customer who doesn't have any heat in her apartment. Complete the conversation with the present perfect or present perfect continuous form of the verbs in parentheses.

Customer Mr. Plansky?

Ken Yes, speaking.

Customer This is Mrs. Morton. I'm so glad I finally got hold of you. _I've been trying_ (try) to call you all day.

Ken I _____ (be) out since early this morning. I _____ (have) a lot of repairs to do because of the cold weather. So, what can I do for you, Mrs. Morton?

Customer Well, the thermostat on our heater _____ (not/work). It _____ (be) off all day.

Ken It doesn't surprise me. I _____ (fix) three thermostats in your building in the last two days. _____ (get) any heat at all?

Customer No, it's freezing in here!

Ken Well, I _____ (finish) my other work for today, so I can come over right away.

Customer Oh, thank you, Mr. Plansky. I really appreciate it.

9 ▶ Complete the conversation between the barber and his customer with the correct form of the verbs in parentheses.

Barber What can I do for you today?

Customer I'd like a haircut. Actually, I just _need_ (need) a trim. Please _____ (not/cut) it too short.

Barber _____ (not/worry) about a thing. You're in good hands. I _____ (cut) hair for years.

Customer Well, the last barber _____ (cut) it too short.

Barber Sir, I _____ (give) more haircuts in the last week than you _____ (have) in your whole life. Trust me, O.K.? I _____ (have) customers—grown men like yourself—who _____ (come) to me since they were children. Even when they _____ (move) away, my customers still _____ (come) back to the old neighborhood for my haircuts. Do you know what one of my customers once _____ (say) to me? "If I _____ (live) 2,000 miles away, I _____ (come) to you for my haircuts on my vacations, anyway!" So sit back and relax.

10 ▶ Ms. Schmidt teaches German to high school students. Read the evaluations she wrote of some of her poorer students. Rewrite each one, beginning it with _If . . . ._

Improvement needed:

1. Mike doesn't make much progress because he doesn't study hard enough. _If Mike studied harder, he'd make more progress._
2. Sue's pronunciation hasn't improved because she never goes to the language laboratory.
3. Louis falls asleep in class because he doesn't get enough sleep at night.
4. Dan has trouble passing his exams because he doesn't do his homework.
5. Janet makes a lot of mistakes because she's always in a hurry.
6. Ann doesn't do well because she misses too many classes.
7. George isn't a better student because he doesn't push himself hard enough.

▶ Work with your classmates. Talk about your English abilities and progress, using _If . . . ._

I think I'd make more progress if I read an English newspaper every day.
If I slowed down a little, I'd probably make fewer mistakes.

▸ Student B follows the instructions below.
▸ Student A follows the instructions on page 122.

Student B Imagine you and your partner are coworkers, and you're trying to set up a one-hour meeting next week. Here is your calendar at work next week. Take turns suggesting times to meet. If your partner suggests a time when you're busy, say what you have to do at that time. Use infinitives.

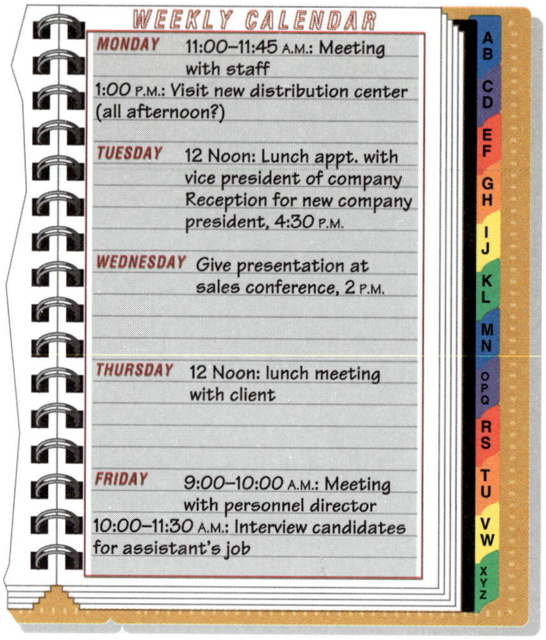

Start like this:

A *How about getting together on Monday at 11:00 am?*
B *I'm sorry, but I have a staff meeting to attend at 11:00. What about 10:00? Can you make it then?*
A *No, I can't. I have some urgent letters to write then.*

11 ▸ **Read the letter.**

WEEKLY CALENDAR

MONDAY	11:00–11:45 A.M.: Meeting with staff
	1:00 P.M.: Visit new distribution center (all afternoon?)
TUESDAY	12 Noon: Lunch appt. with vice president of company
	Reception for new company president, 4:30 P.M.
WEDNESDAY	Give presentation at sales conference, 2 P.M.
THURSDAY	12 Noon: lunch meeting with client
FRIDAY	9:00–10:00 A.M.: Meeting with personnel director
	10:00–11:30 A.M.: Interview candidates for assistant's job

April 15th

Dear Chris,
I've been meaning to write to you for a long time, but I've been so busy with school that I haven't had a free minute. Besides going to school full time, I've also been working at a part-time job on weekends—I've been driving a taxi! I only started last month, and I've worked three weekends so far. I've been getting pretty good tips, so the money's O.K. One advantage is that I've been practicing my English with the passengers!
How have you been? What have you been doing since I last saw you? Please send news. If you're ever in this part of the world, I hope you'll visit.

Best wishes,

Miki

▸ **Now write your own letter to a friend. Include the information below.**

Say that you've been meaning to write and explain why you haven't.
Tell your friend what you've been doing lately. Give some details.
Ask how your friend has been and ask what he/she has been doing.
Say that you'd like to see your friend or hear from him/her.

12 ▸ **Listen to the first part of each conversation and choose the best response.**

1. a. I'll travel around the world.
   b. I'd travel around the world.

2. a. I've been playing a lot of tennis.
   b. I played a lot of tennis.

3. a. O.K. If I have time next week, I'll give you a call.
   b. O.K. If I had time next week, I'd give you a call.

4. a. Not unless I go to the mountains.
   b. Not if the weather isn't nice.

5. a. Yes, that's a good idea.
   b. Yes, I feel fine.

6. a. No, I had trouble falling asleep.
   b. No, I've been having trouble falling asleep.

7. a. She told me to get plenty of rest.
   b. She said so.

8. a. I'd better not move.
   b. You'd better not move.

9. a. Not if you don't want to.
   b. Not if you don't have to.

10. a. You don't have to sit here unless you have a ticket.
    b. You're not supposed to sit here unless you have a ticket.

PREVIEW

FUNCTIONS/THEMES	LANGUAGE	FORMS
Ask for information	Do you know if there's a bank around here? Yes, there's one on the next block. I wonder if they exchange currency.	Embedded yes-no questions
Ask for travel information	Could you tell me if there are any inexpensive tours?	
Correct a mistaken impression	I thought you were Mexican. I *am* Mexican. No, I'm Spanish.	Sequence of tenses
Talk about food	Have you ever had *paella*? Yes, I have. I thought it was delicious. No, I haven't. What is it? It's a rice dish made with seafood, chicken, and spices. It's cooked slowly in a large pan.	
Make an objection	It's too hot to go for a walk. I don't have enough energy to go for a walk.	*Too . . . to* and *not . . . enough . . . to*

Preview the conversations.

Tourist Tips
HOURS IN MADRID

The following hours of opening and closing are approximate and are observed by many business establishments. However, hours can vary widely, so check first.

banks	8:30 A.M. to 2:00 P.M. (Mon.–Fri.); 8:30 A.M. to 1:00 P.M. (Sat.)
shops	10:00 A.M. to 1:30 P.M. and 5:00 P.M. to 8:00 P.M. (some closed Sat. afternoons)
restaurants	1:30 P.M. to 4:00 P.M. and 9:00 P.M. to midnight
cafés	8:00 A.M. to well after midnight
museums	9:30 A.M. to 2:00 P.M. and 4:00 P.M. to 7:00 P.M. (some open at midday; many closed Mon.)

It's a Tuesday in May. Jane, Kathy, and Bob arrived in Madrid early this morning, and they have spent the whole time until two o'clock at the Prado Museum. Read the section from the guidebook called "Hours in Madrid." Then work with a partner and figure out if Jane, Kathy, and Bob will be able to do all of the things listed below. Why or why not?

1. Jane wants to change some money at the bank.
2. Kathy wants to go to some small shops to look for gifts.
3. Bob wants to go have lunch.

75. It's too early to have dinner.

The Smiths are on vacation in Spain. They arrived in Madrid yesterday.

A

Mr. Smith Well, now we've seen the famous Prado.

Mrs. Smith It's a fabulous museum, isn't it?

Peter Smith Yeah, it really is. But it's been a long day, and I'm starving.

Mrs. Smith It's only seven. It's too early to have dinner. The restaurants don't open till nine, but we could find a café and get some coffee.

Mr. Smith I think we should go to the Museum of Fine Arts. I wonder if it's still open.

Peter Smith I don't have enough energy to stand up, let alone go to another museum.

Mrs. Smith Is it far? I don't know if I can walk much more, either.

Peter Smith I thought we were going to get something to drink.

Mr. Smith Well, while you're having your coffee, I'll see if there's a bus to the museum. *(Looking in guidebook)* Now, how do you say "museum"? . . .

Figure it out

1. Listen to the conversations and write:
   - √ next to the things the Smiths have done today.
   - + next to the things they're planning to do today.
   - × next to the things they aren't going to do today.

   _√_ see the Prado Museum
   ____ find a café to have something to drink
   ____ take a bus to another museum
   ____ go to the Museum of Fine Arts
   ____ have *paella* for dinner

2. Listen to the conversations again and say *True, False,* or *It doesn't say.*

1. The Smiths can have dinner in a restaurant after nine o'clock.
2. Peter wants to do more sightseeing today.
3. The Museum of Fine Arts probably isn't open after seven.
4. The man in the café speaks English at work.
5. *Paella* is a fried chicken dish.

Mr. Smith Uh . . . *Señor* . . .
Man in café I speak English.
Mr. Smith Oh . . . I thought you were Spanish.
Man in café I *am* Spanish. But I speak English too.
Mr. Smith Do you know if there's a bus to the Museum of Fine Arts?
Man in café Most likely. I doubt if the museum is open at this hour, though.
Mr. Smith Hmm . . . I thought it might be too late to go.
Mrs. Smith Let's just sit here and enjoy the café. Maybe we can go have *paella* for dinner later on.
Peter Smith *Paella?* What's that?
Mrs. Smith *(Reading from guidebook)* It's a rice dish made with seafood, chicken, and spices. It's cooked slowly in a large pan.
Peter Smith It sounds good. Let's try it.
Man in café I remember the way my grandmother used to make it. It was really delicious.

3. Find another way to say it.

1. I'm very hungry.
2. I'll find out if there's a bus to the museum.
3. Probably.
4. I don't think the museum is open this late, though.
5. Aren't we going to get something to drink?

76. Do you know if there's a bank around here?

1 ▶ Listen to the conversations and circle the places on the map that the speakers are looking for.

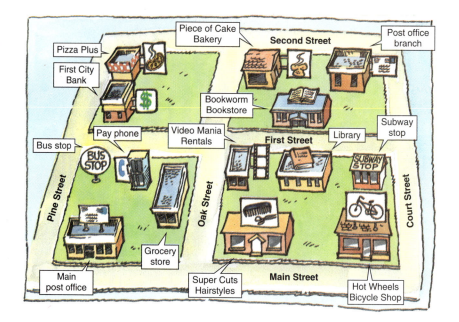

2 ▶ Listen to the two possible conversations and practice them with a partner.
▶ Act out similar conversations. Use the places on the map in exercise 1 and the information in the box.

A Do you know if there's a bank around here?

B Yes, there's one on the next block.   **B** Sorry, but I can't think of one.
A I wonder if they exchange currency.
B I doubt it.

Some information

At some banks, they exchange currency.
Some banks are open in the evenings.
At some bicycle shops, they do repairs.
Some post offices have passport applications.
For some hairstylists, you need an appointment.

3 ▶ Study the frames: Embedded yes-no questions

		Is there a bank around here?	
		Are they open late?	
		Do they exchange currency?	Short answers
Do you know		there's a bank around here?	I'm not sure if there is.
Could you tell me	if	they're open late?	I doubt if they are.
I wonder		they exchange currency.	I don't know if they do.

4 ▶ Work with a partner. Take turns asking and answering questions about the places or things in your building, neighborhood, town, or city. Use embedded questions to ask about the location and then ask for additional information.

A *Do you know if there's a vending machine in this building?*
B *I think there's one on the second floor.*
A *I wonder if it gives change.*

Some places and things	Information
a coffee/vending machine	give change?
a public phone	take phone cards?
a subway station	run all night?
a library	open on weekends?
a video-rental store	carry music videos?
a photocopy shop	send faxes?

5 ▶ **A man is calling a hotel to make a reservation. Listen to the conversation and answer the questions on his list.**

Questions: International Hotel

Business rate? *$100/night*
Airport transportation?
Business center in hotel?
Check-in time?
Late checkout?
Restaurants?

6 ▶ **Complete the telephone conversation. Combine each pair of sentences in brackets [ ] into one sentence.**
▶ **Listen to check your work.**

Travel agent Thank you for calling Travel Options. Sophia speaking. How can I help you?

Customer Hello. I'd like some information about your winter package tours to the Caribbean. [Are there any inexpensive tours? Could you tell me?] *Could you tell me if there are any inexpensive tours?*

Travel agent All our tours are very reasonable, but the least expensive ones are the "Long Weekend Package Trips." You leave on a Thursday and get back on Monday.

Customer Well, I haven't quite decided when I'll be going. . . . I'm interested in Puerto Rico. [Is it offered in that package? Do you know?]

Travel agent Yes, Puerto Rico is one of the destinations offered in that package. [Are you planning to go in January? Do you know?]

Customer Yes, probably around the end of January.

Travel agent That's the best time to get away from the cold weather. The islands are beautiful then.

Customer I'm sure they are. [Are the hotels any good? Do you know?]

Travel agent Absolutely! The hotels have been inspected by our own agents.

Customer Uh-huh. [Would I have to pay for anything besides the package? Could you tell me?]

Travel agent The package includes *everything*: airfare, airport transportation, hotel accommodations with meals, and a free scuba diving lesson. You even get a complimentary pineapple juice drink on arrival!

7 ▶ **Work with a partner. Play these roles.**

Student A You'd like to make a reservation at the Gateway Hotel, and you also have some questions. Your partner is a receptionist there. Ask your partner the questions in the box below, beginning them with *Could you tell me if . . . ?* or *Do you know if . . . ?*

Some questions

Do you have a double room for tomorrow night?
Does the room have a good view?
Is there a restaurant in the hotel?
Will the room be ready at noon?

A *Hello. I'd like to make a reservation. Could you tell me if you have a double room for tomorrow night? . . .*

Student B You're a receptionist at the Gateway Hotel. Your partner would like to make a reservation and has some questions. Answer his or her questions, using the information in the box below. If you're not sure of something, begin your answer with *I'm not sure if . . . .*

Some information

There's a double room available for tomorrow night.
It might not have a good view.
The hotel doesn't have a restaurant.
Rooms usually aren't ready until 3:00 P.M.

77. I thought you were Mexican.

1 ► Listen to the two possible conversations and
   practice them with a partner.
   ► Act out similar conversations, using the sentences
   in the box or your own ideas.

A I thought you were Mexican.

B I *am* Mexican.   **B** No, I'm Spanish.

I thought . . .
you were Mexican.
you taught Spanish.
Chinese was your native language.
you had three children.
we were having a test today.

Normal form	Emphatic form
I'm Mexican.	I *am* Mexican.
I teach Spanish.	I *do* teach Spanish.

2 ► Study the frames: Sequence of tenses

Simple present	Present or future tense		Simple past	Past tense form
I **think**	he**'s** Canadian.		I **thought**	he **was** Canadian.
I **know**	he **speaks** French.		I **knew**	he **spoke** some French.
I **don't think**	he**'s studying** English.		I **didn't think**	he **was studying** English.
I **know**	he **can understand** French.		I **knew**	he **could understand** French.
I**'m** sure	he**'ll help** us.		I **was** sure	he**'d help** us.
I **think**	he **may know** what to do.		I **thought**	he **might know** what to do.

Even though these forms are in the past, the meaning is still present or future. Notice that *could* is the past of *can, would* is the past of *will,* and *might* is the past of *may.* The modal auxiliaries use the same form for all pronouns.

3 ► Complete the letter with the correct form of the verbs in parentheses.

Dear Lisa,

    I was so surprised to get your letter. I didn't know you <u>were</u>
<u>looking for</u> (look for) an apartment here in Seattle. In fact, I had no
idea you _____ (think) of moving here. I thought you _____ (like)
California too much to ever leave, but I guess you felt it _____ (be)
time for a change. When are you supposed to start your new job? You'll
have to tell me all about it.

    Anyway, I called my brother right away because I thought maybe he
_____ (can) help you find an apartment. He thought there _____ (may)
be a vacant apartment in his building, but he wasn't sure it _____
(be) still available. As soon as I have any information, I'll let you
know.

    Please call or write if you need help with anything else.

                Best,

                Barbara

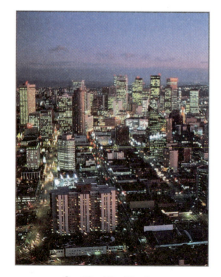

Seattle, Washington

78. Have you ever had *paella*?

1 ▶ **Listen to the two possible conversations and practice them with a partner.**

A Have you ever had *paella*?

B No, I haven't. What is it?

A It's a rice dish made with seafood, chicken, and spices. It's cooked slowly in a large pan.

B Mmm! It sounds wonderful.

B Yes, I have. I thought it was delicious.

Paella

INGREDIENTS

2 large red bell peppers	6 large cloves of garlic, chopped
2 tbs. olive oil	3 lbs. tomatoes, peeled, seeded, and chopped
4 oz. chorizo	12–16 mussels or clams
1 4-lb. chicken, cut into pieces	6 cups chicken stock
3 teas. salt	1 lb. peas
2 teas. black pepper	3 cups short-grain rice
1 lb. pork, diced	1 teas. saffron threads or 1/2 teas. powdered saffron
12–16 large prawns or shrimp in their shells	
1 lb. squid	8 lemon wedges

2 ▶ **Work with a partner. Take turns describing a dish you like to eat or cook, or both. Talk about the ingredients and how the dish is made.**

Some cooking terms

It's cooked in a large pan.
It's baked in the oven.
It's fried in oil.
It's boiled.
It's sautéed in butter.
It's served with rice.

Some ingredients

oysters	pork
scallops	beans
fish	spinach
beef	garlic
chicken	hot peppers
lamb	coconut

MAKE AN OBJECTION • *TOO . . . TO* AND *NOT . . . ENOUGH . . . TO*

3 ▶ **Listen to the two possible conversations and practice them with a partner.**
▶ **Act out similar conversations, using *too . . . to* and *not . . . enough . . . to*.**

A Let's go for a walk.

B It's too hot to go for a walk.

B I don't have enough energy to go for a walk.

Some suggestions	Some reasons to object
go for a walk	It's very hot outside.
go out for dinner	It's only 4:00 P.M.
go get some coffee	You have to be somewhere in fifteen minutes.
go to a museum	You're tired.
go to a movie	You have almost no money.

4 ▶ **Work with a partner. Take turns making suggestions (for example, what to do after class or on the weekend, where to have a meal, or any other ideas you have). Think of an objection to every one of your partner's suggestions, using *too . . . to* or *not . . . enough . . . to*.**

How about going for a run in the park?

No, I'm too tired to go running.

79. Somehow, I doubt it.

It's Monday, and Anita and Ed are having lunch together at a café.

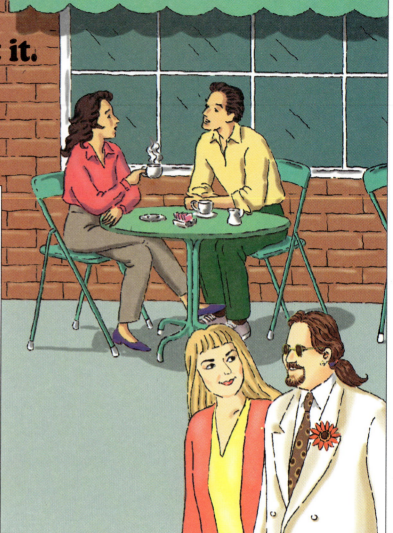

1

Anita I still can't get over the burglary at the Kims' house.

Ed From what you've told me, it must have happened sometime Saturday evening.

Anita Yes. In fact, it could only have happened during a two-hour period. Dr. Kim and her family left the house just before five, and they stopped back a little after seven.

Ed Do the Kims have any idea how the burglars got in?

Anita Well, that's the most mysterious part. The police checked the whole house, but they couldn't find any clues. It was almost as if the thieves had a key and locked up on their way out.

Ed It doesn't start to get dark until around seven, so they must not have looked suspicious. . . . Do you know if Kate came to our place with Lou today?

Anita No, I don't. . . . But somehow, I doubt it.

Ed No, wait—we're jumping to conclusions. This isn't the first time a house in this town has been broken into. We don't have enough facts to make a judgment.

Anita You're right. I suppose we should give her the benefit of the doubt. Still, there *have* been a lot of coincidences.

2. Figure it out

Check (√) the statements that are said or implied in the conversation.

1. ___ The Kims' house was burglarized on Saturday.
2. ___ The burglary took place shortly before five o'clock.
3. ___ The thieves probably looked suspicious.
4. ___ Anita suspects that maybe Kate took their mask and also robbed the Kims.
5. ___ Anita and Ed both left the apartment this morning before Lou got there.
6. ___ Ed thinks Kate is innocent of the crimes.

3. Listen in

Mike, a friend of the Riveras', joins them at the café for coffee. They are all trying to make plans. Read the questions below. Then listen to the conversation and answer the questions.

1. What would Mike like to do tonight?
2. What might he have to do tonight?
3. What might he do tomorrow night?

80. Your turn

Look at the pictures. Where do you think they were taken?
You may look up the answers on page 165.
If you could visit one of these places, which one would you choose? Why?

Here are some reasons why people like to take vacations in other countries.
Work in groups and discuss which of these would be the most important for you.

- to shop
- to meet new people
- to see how other people live
- to learn about the history of a country
- to do something exciting
- to practice speaking a foreign language
- to get away from problems at home
- to relax
- to seem more interesting to people
- to sightsee
- to be in a different climate

How to say it

Practice the conversation.

A Someone told me you were from Chile.

B I *am* from Chile.

A But you don't speak Spanish.

B I *do* speak Spanish. I just don't speak it here at work.

81.

PAUL THEROUX

What do you think it takes to be a good traveler? What's the difference between a vacationer and an explorer? Read the article to find out this author's point of view.

Writer Paul Theroux has become famous for his books about his train travels. *The Great Railway Bazaar* is the story of his trip across Asia, and *The Old Patagonian Express* describes his journey from Boston to the tip of South America. Recently, he spoke to *GEO* magazine about his philosophy of travel. Theroux believes that there is still much out there to see if you are willing to open your eyes and undergo a little risk and hardship.

GEO:

There's a tradition of a grand tour, a journey that teaches young people about the important cultures of their time. What should today's grand tour be?

THEROUX:

People should travel not only to find out about the present but to find out about the future. A grand tour today should be the opposite of what it was in the past. Travelers should avoid museums, cathedrals, castles, and ruins. They should go where human life is, to places that give them an image of the future.

GEO:

What does it take to be a good traveler?

THEROUX:

Courage. Curiosity. Travelers have to be alone. They have to take risks. And they have to be among things vastly different from those they have come from. You see, a lot of people who travel are only looking for an idealized version of home. They travel to find home with better food, home plus more sunshine, home plus easier parking, home plus no crime, home plus the possibility of romance. The point is, they're not looking for very much. They're not looking for the foreign, the strange, the really outlandish. People have always traveled in two ways. There have always been explorers, and there have always been vacationers. The explorer has the instinct to be the first person to see something, or the last. Only explorers will tell you this, but it's a fact: There are many, many places on earth where no one has ever been. The fact is, there are parts of the Amazon where animals will walk up and lick your hand because they've never seen a human being before. You can still see things as strange as Columbus ever saw.

---

1. Read the article. Then check (√) the statements which are Theroux's opinions.

1. ___ A modern grand tour should include visits to museums and cathedrals.
2. ___ People should travel in groups.
3. ___ A good traveler has to be willing to go to places that are strange and unusual.
4. ___ An explorer tries to find places that no one has ever been to.
5. ___ Good travelers look for places that will give them a picture of the future.

2. Say *Same* or *Different*.

1. outlandish
   usual
2. trip
   journey
3. hardship
   difficulty
4. avoid
   look for
5. take a risk
   take a chance
6. image
   picture

3. What kinds of places do you think Theroux enjoys visiting? Do you agree with Theroux's point of view? Do you think there are other good reasons to travel besides the ones he discusses?

PREVIEW

FUNCTIONS/THEMES	LANGUAGE	FORMS
Identify something	Could I see that shirt, please? Which one? The plaid one.	
Ask about material	What's this blouse made of? It's 100 percent silk.	
Ask for advice	I'm looking for a gift for my sister-in-law, but I'm not sure what to get her. Do you know if she has any hobbies? Do you know what her hobbies are?	Embedded questions: yes-no questions vs. information questions
Express a concern	What if he doesn't like it?	
Express a regret Make a judgment	I guess I should have looked it over more carefully. He should have tried them on in the store.	*Should have*

Preview the conversations.

Student A
You want to buy a gift for a friend or a relative, but you're having trouble thinking of ideas. Describe the person to Student B and ask for advice.

Student B
Student A wants to buy a gift for someone and asks your advice. Find out about the person the gift is for by asking questions about his or her interests. Then make suggestions.

82. What if . . . ?

Larry is helping Mark buy a gift for a new friend of his.

A

Mark I really appreciate your coming with me, Larry. I have so much trouble picking out gifts.

Larry Well, take your time. Look around, and maybe you'll get inspired.

B

Saleswoman May I help you?

Mark I'm trying to buy a gift for a friend, but I'm not sure what to get her.

Saleswoman Well, these sweaters are lovely. They're a real value for the money.

Mark Hmm . . . I'm not sure. . . . Could I see that striped one on the bottom shelf?

Saleswoman This one?

Mark No, the one with the blue stripes.

Saleswoman You have good taste, sir. This is a beauty. It's 100 percent wool. It's also the latest style.

Larry It's nice, Mark.

Mark I don't know. What if Carol doesn't like stripes? . . .

Larry Oh, I'm sure she'll like it.

Saleswoman Do you know what size your friend wears?

Mark Uh, no, I don't. *(Laughs nervously)* I guess I should have found out.

C

Larry How about something for her apartment? Do you know if Carol likes to cook?

Mark I don't think she does. Besides, I don't have the slightest idea what she needs.

Larry Do you know what kind of music she likes?

Mark Classical, I think. Hmm . . . maybe I'll get her a CD.

D

Larry Well, I think you made an excellent choice. . . . Mark?

Mark Oh, did you say something?

Larry Are you happy with what you bought?

Mark Well, I don't know now. . . . Maybe I shouldn't have bought her a CD. I mean, what if she doesn't have a CD player?

Figure it out

1. Listen to the conversations and say *True, False*, or *It doesn't say*.

1. Mark is shopping for a gift for Carol's birthday.
2. Mark has trouble making decisions.
3. Mark doesn't know very much about Carol.
4. Mark bought Carol a sweater.
5. Mark thinks Carol likes classical music.
6. Mark isn't sure he made the right decision.
7. Carol doesn't have a CD player.

2. Find another way to say it.

1. It's all wool.
2. Don't hurry.
3. I have so much trouble choosing gifts.
4. Carol might not like stripes.
5. It's too bad I didn't find out.
6. Does Carol like to cook?

83. What's it made of?

1 ▶ Listen to the conversations in a store and check (√) the item that each shopper is asking about.

1

2

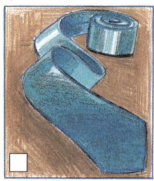

3

4

2 ▶ Listen to the conversation and practice it with a partner.
▶ Act out similar conversations, using the pictures in exercise 1.

A Could I see that shirt, please?
B Which one?
A The plaid one.

ASK ABOUT MATERIAL

3 ▶ Listen to the two possible conversations and practice them with a partner.
▶ Act out similar conversations. Ask about the items in exercise 1.

A What's this blouse made of?

B It's made of silk.   **B** It's 100 percent silk.

Some kinds of material	
cotton	silk
wool	leather

4 ▶ **Study the frame:**
Embedded questions:
yes-no questions vs.
information questions

	Does she **have** any hobbies?
	What **are** her hobbies?
	What size **does** she **wear**?
Do you know	if she **has** any hobbies?
	what her hobbies **are**?
	what size she **wears**?

5 ▶ **Listen to the two possible conversations and practice them with a partner.**
▶ **Act out similar conversations, using the information in the box.**

A I'm looking for a gift for my sister-in-law, but I'm not sure what to get her.

B Do you know if she has any hobbies?

A She plays tennis, collects butterflies, and is interested in photography.

B Why don't you get her . . . ?

B Do you know what her hobbies are?

A I don't have the slightest idea.

B Well, do you know . . . ?

Some questions

Does she have any hobbies?/
 What are her hobbies?
Does she have a CD player?
What kind of music does she like?
Does she wear wool sweaters?
What size does she wear?

6 ▶ **Rewrite the questions in brackets [ ], using the expressions from the box. (Sometimes there is more than one possible question.) Then complete Dan's part of the conversation, using the information in the page from the clothing catalogue.**
▶ **Practice the conversation with a partner.**

Do you know . . . ?
Do you have any idea . . . ?
Could I ask you . . . ?
Do you remember . . . ?
Does it say . . . ?

Tom I really like your shirt. [Where did you get it?]
Do you remember where you got it?

Dan I ordered it from Outdoor World.

Tom [Can you still get them?]

Dan I'm sure you can.

Tom [How much was it?]

Dan It wasn't that expensive. But that was three years ago. Let's look in this year's catalogue. . . . Here it is—the Men's Alpine Hiking Shirt.

Tom [How much does it cost?]

Dan _____

Tom [What's it made of?]

Dan _____

Tom [Does it come in solid colors?]

Dan _____

Tom [Do they make them for children?]

Dan _____

Alpine Hiking Shirt

A practical, medium-weight shirt. Made of 85% pure wool with 15% nylon added for strength. Handsome plaid or solid colors. Dry clean.

1483H Men's Alpine Hiking Shirt. Sizes: Sm., Med., Lg., XLg. Plaid or solid (green, navy blue). **$39.95**

4752H Women's Alpine Hiking Shirt. Sizes: Sm., Med., Lg., XLg. Plaid or solid (green). **$39.95**

4721H Children's Alpine Hiking Shirt. Sizes: Sm., Med., Lg., XLg. Plaid only. **$29.95**

84. What if he doesn't like it?

1 ▶ Listen to the conversation and practice it with a partner.
▶ Act out similar conversations, using the information in the boxes.

A I finally got my brother a birthday present yesterday.
B You did? Great!
A But what if he doesn't like it?
B Oh, I'm sure he will.

> Use a present tense form after the expression *What if . . . ?* when you are talking about the future.
>
> What if he *doesn't* like it? = Maybe he *won't* like it.

Some situations
I finally got my brother a birthday present yesterday.
I've finished my last paper for this term.
I was offered two different jobs this week.
My sister has agreed to stay in my apartment while I'm away.
My son was just accepted into college.

Some worries
Maybe I'll make the wrong decision.
Maybe she'll change her mind.
Maybe he won't like it.
Maybe he won't want to go.
Maybe I won't do well on my final exams.

2 ▶ Read the letter and change the sentences in brackets [ ] to questions, using *What if . . . ?*

I've been going out with a woman I met a few months ago. It's getting serious, and I want to ask her to marry me.
  The trouble is that I really don't know much about her, except that she comes from Australia. [Maybe she'll decide to go back there.] I haven't met her family yet. [Maybe they won't like me.] And most important, I'm not sure she feels the same way about me. [Maybe she'll turn me down.] I'm so worried that I just can't make a decision. What do you think?

Arthur

3 ▶ Work with a partner. Imagine you are the person in each picture. Tell your partner about your worries, using *What if . . . ?*

What if there's a storm?

4 ▶ Work with a partner. Think of some things you are worried about in the future. Tell your partner about them, using *What if . . . ?*

I'm planning to go to the beach next weekend. What if it rains?
I've applied to four universities. What if I don't get into any of them?

85. I should have looked it over more carefully.

1 ▶ **Listen to the conversation and practice it with a partner.**
   ▶ **Act out similar conversations, using the information in the boxes.**

A Doesn't your sweater have a hole in it?
B I guess I should have looked it over more
   carefully.

Some doubts	Some regrets
Doesn't your sweater have a hole in it?	I shouldn't have gotten her another one.
Aren't those shoes too big for you?	I shouldn't have bought him a CD.
John doesn't have a CD player, does he?	I should have looked it over more carefully.
Maria already has two cats, doesn't she?	I should have tried them on.

2 ▶ **Study the frame:** *Should have*

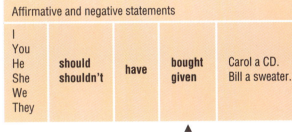

Use *should have* to express a regret or to make a judgment about something that happened in the past.

Affirmative and negative statements

I You He She We They	should shouldn't	have	bought given	Carol a CD. Bill a sweater.

▲ past participle

3 ▶ **Read the following situations and make at least two judgments about each one— one with *should have* and one with *shouldn't have*.**

1. Jack bought a pair of shoes in five minutes, without trying them on. At home, he found out that they were too small.
   He should have tried them on in the store. He shouldn't have . . .

2. Susan asked her mother to buy her a blouse. When her mother brought it home, Susan didn't like the color or the style.

3. Pam borrowed a tape recorder for a class she was teaching. During the class, she couldn't figure out how it worked.

4. Sam rented the first apartment he looked at. The next day, he found a much better one, but it was too late.

4 ▶ **Listen to the two conversations. Write two things that the first speaker in each conversation regrets. Use *should have* and *shouldn't have*. Compare your answers with your classmates' answers.**

Conversation 1	Conversation 2
1.	1.
2.	2.

5 ▶ **Can you think of something you've done in the past that you now regret? Tell your classmates about it.**

I shouldn't have left home at such a young age.
I should have studied harder when I was in high school.

86. I tried calling you . . .

It's Tuesday morning, and Lou has just arrived at the Riveras' house for work.

1

Anita Good morning, Lou. Still no Kate?

Lou Still no Kate and still no word.

Anita What if something's happened to her?

Lou I wouldn't worry. She's probably O.K.

Anita It seems like one thing after another. You know that the Kims' house was broken into, don't you?

Lou No, I didn't know. When did *that* happen?

Anita Saturday. But maybe now that things are taking a turn for the better . . .

Lou They are?

Anita Oh, that's right. You don't know the *good* news yet. I tried calling you last night, but you must have been out.

Lou I was home. The phone didn't ring once.

Anita Maybe there's something wrong with your phone, then. Anyway, we found the mask.

Lou That *is* good news! Where was it?

Anita Well, you know that Ed's sister and her family were staying with us for a few days? It turns out that her daughter, Lisa, was playing with the neighborhood kids, and they took the mask into the room she was staying in. They were playing and just forgot about it.

Lou Oh, no! She has good taste, that kid!

Anita She didn't even realize that Ed and I were looking for it.

Lou Well, that's one "crime" solved.

Anita More than that. They solved the "dancer crimes" too, you know.

Lou Oh, they got them?

Anita Yes. Three women danced all the way to jail. They caught them breaking into the house next door to the Kims'.

2. Figure it out

Say *True*, *False*, or *It doesn't say*.

1. Lou hasn't heard from Kate.
2. Anita is worried that maybe something has happened to Kate.
3. When Lou heard about the break-in at the Kims', he immediately thought of Kate.
4. Lou's phone was busy Monday evening.
5. The mask was in Lisa's room.
6. Lisa knew that her aunt and uncle were looking for the mask.
7. The police are still looking for the "dancer criminals."

3. Listen in

Anita and Lou continue their conversation. Read the questions below. Then listen to the conversation and answer the questions.

1. What does Anita think she shouldn't have done?
2. What two things does Anita think she should have done?

87. Your turn

Look at the photos and descriptions below. Then read the gift ideas. In groups, decide what you think would be an appropriate gift for each of these people. You may use the gift ideas suggested or your own ideas.

Susan
A nineteen-year-old college student
Interests: Enjoys pop music, dancing; likes to eat, but hates to cook
Occasion: Just moved into her first apartment

Steve
A twenty-five-year-old French teacher
Interests: Likes to travel during school vacations
Occasion: His birthday

Martha
A thirty-year-old travel agent
Interests: Painting, movies, computers
Occasion: Just started a new job

Bill
A sixty-five-year-old business executive
Interests: Cooking, golf
Occasion: His retirement

Some Gift Ideas

Food Cheeses, jams and jellies, nuts, cookies, candy, fresh fruit, baked goods, exotic or regional foods, selected sauces, selected teas, coffees

For travel Tote bag, folding umbrella, sewing kit, stationery and stamps, travel iron, passport case, diary, alarm clock, dictionary of foreign terms, regional guide, travel game

For the office Clock for desk or wall, letter opener, briefcase, pocket calculator, desk calendar, pen and pencil set, dictionary/thesaurus set, large standing plant, bookends

For the home Kitchen accessories (cooking equipment, cookbook, knife set, cutting board), bath or beach towels, guest soaps, serving tray, CDs or tapes, specialty gadgets, food or drink

For a special occasion (recognition, retirement . . .) Tie clip or brooch, watch or bracelet, clock, scrapbook (with pictures already mounted), tickets for an event, works of art (a framed painting or poster), a hobby or sports item (painting, golf, tennis)

For someone who is ill Amusing book, flowering plant, taped music or book, cologne, game, robe, slippers, card or cassette tape with individual good wishes from group members, recorded VCR tapes

For sensitive giving (death, serious injury . . .) Appropriate book for the time, fresh flowers, large plant, taped music, personal letter or card

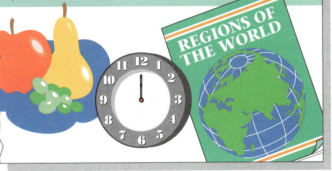

Think of someone you might give a gift to in the next six months. Describe the person to your classmates. What are his/her interests? What is the occasion? How much money do you plan to spend on the gift, or would you rather make the gift yourself? Your classmates will help you decide on a gift.

How to say it

Practice the phrases. Then practice the conversation.

should have [ʃúdəv]   shouldn't have [ʃúdntəv]

A I feel terrible. I shouldn't have eaten all those french fries.
B And you shouldn't have eaten two pieces of chocolate cake for dessert.
A You're right. I should have had some fruit instead.

88.

The Gift

O. Henry (1862–1910) was a famous American short story writer. The story here is adapted from one of his most famous works, "The Gift of the Magi."

One dollar and eighty-seven cents. Three times Della counted it. One dollar and eighty-seven cents. And the next day would be Christmas.

Della had been saving every penny she could for months. Twenty dollars a week doesn't go very far. Expenses had been greater than she had calculated. They always are. Now she had only $1.87 to buy a present for Jim. Her Jim. And what could she do with such a small amount of money?

Suddenly she turned to the mirror. Her eyes were shining brilliantly, but her face had lost its color. Rapidly she pulled down her hair and let it fall to its full length.

Now there were two possessions in which she and Jim both took a mighty pride. One was Jim's gold watch that had been his father's and his grandfather's. The other was Della's hair.

So now Della's beautiful hair fell around her, rippling and shining like water. It reached below her knee and made itself almost a garment for her. And then she did it up again nervously and quickly.

On went her old brown jacket. On went her old brown hat. She left the apartment and ran down the stairs to the street.

She stopped where the sign read: "Madame Sofronie. Hair Goods of All Kinds." Up the stairs she ran.

"Will you buy my hair?" asked Della.

"Twenty dollars," said Madame, lifting the long hair with a practiced hand.

"Give it to me quickly," said Della.

For the next two hours, Della searched the stores for Jim's present. And she found it at last, a beautiful gold watch chain. Twenty-one dollars they took from her, and she hurried home with 87 cents.

Jim was never late, and Della waited nervously for him to arrive. Suddenly, the door opened and Jim stepped in. When he saw Della, he stopped, as unmoving as a dog that smells a bird.

"Jim, darling," she cried, "don't look at me that way. I sold my hair because I couldn't have lived through Christmas without giving you a present. Don't you still like me just as well?"

Jim seemed to wake quickly out of his trance. He hugged Della and then pulled a package from his overcoat pocket and threw it on the table. Inside, Della found an expensive set of combs for her vanished hair.

"Never mind, Jim," she said. "My hair will grow quickly." And then she leaped up like a cat. Jim had not yet seen his beautiful present. She held the chain out to him eagerly. "Give me your watch," she cried. "I want to see how it looks on it!"

1. **Read the story. The last few lines are missing. How do you think the story ends? Discuss your answer with your classmates. Then read the missing lines on page 165.**

2. **Writers sometimes put words in an unusual order to make their style of writing more interesting. Rephrase these sentences by changing the word order. For some items, additional changes may be necessary.**

1. Three times Della counted it.
   Della counted it three times.
2. Rapidly she pulled down her hair.
3. On went her old brown jacket.
4. On went her old brown hat.
5. Up the stairs she ran.
6. Twenty-one dollars they took from her.

FUNCTIONS/THEMES	LANGUAGE	FORMS
State a possibility in the past	I wonder what's keeping Ed. He may/might have gotten lost. He may/might not have understood your directions.	*May have* and *might have*
State a conclusion about the past	He must not have written down the time.	*Must have*
React to a situation	They may have gotten stuck in traffic. They might have left the house late. They must have had an accident.	*May have*, *might have*, and *must have*
Give an excuse	You were supposed to be here at noon. The bus broke down, so I had to walk.	*Be supposed to* vs. *have to* in the past
Report a conversation	Did you tell him (that) I had an appointment at 3:30? Yes, and he said (that) he'd meet us for lunch at 2:00.	Direct and reported speech

Preview the conversations.

Student A

Imagine you work for an international company. You and a coworker, George Stern, are both visiting Rio de Janeiro, Brazil, for a business conference. Student B is your Brazilian sales representative. Call Student B and arrange a lunch meeting.

1. Find out if Student B can meet you and George at two o'clock tomorrow.
2. Tell Student B that George has another appointment at three thirty that he has to be on time for.
3. Suggest meeting at the Jardim Restaurant on República do Perú.

Student B

Imagine you are a sales representative in Rio de Janeiro, Brazil. Two people from your company (Student A and a coworker, George Stern) are in town for a few days. Student A calls you to arrange a lunch meeting. Answer Student A's questions.

1. You're free for lunch every day this week, and any time is fine.
2. You know where the Jardim Restaurant is because you were just there yesterday.

89. He said he'd be here at two.

Judy and George have made an appointment to meet Sam for lunch.
They are waiting for Sam at the Jardim Restaurant in Rio de Janeiro, Brazil.

A

Judy I wonder what's keeping Sam. He was supposed to be here at two.

George Did you tell him I had to be back by three thirty?

Judy Yes, I told him that you had an appointment that you couldn't be late for. He said he'd be here at two o'clock sharp.

George It's already two thirty.

Judy I know. Stop pacing like that. You're making me nervous.

George Do you think he might have gotten lost? He may not have understood your directions.

Judy I didn't have to give him any directions. He said he knew where the place was. He must not have written down the time.

George It just isn't like him to be late, though.

Judy I'm sure there's a logical explanation. Something must have come up.

George Well, it makes no sense for me to wait any longer. I think I'll just grab a bite to eat and get back.

Judy O.K. I'll stay here and wait for him.

Figure it out

1. Listen to the conversations and check (√) the sentences that are stated or implied.

1. _____ George is worried about missing his appointment.
2. _____ Sam had trouble understanding Judy's directions.
3. _____ Sam didn't write down the time of the appointment.
4. _____ Sam is often late.
5. _____ George and Judy waited until Sam arrived.
6. _____ Sam arrived more than half an hour late.
7. _____ The bus had a flat tire.
8. _____ Sam tried to get a taxi.
9. _____ Sam wasn't planning to walk.

Judy There you are! It's ten to three. What happened?

Sam Hi! I'm sorry I'm so late. The bus broke down. I couldn't get another one or a taxi, so I had to walk. Where's George?

Judy He had an appointment to go to. He had to be there at three thirty, remember?

Sam Oh, I'm really sorry. I'll have to apologize to George when I see him.

2. Find another way to say it.

1. He isn't usually late, though.
2. He probably didn't write down the time.
3. I'll just eat something fast.
4. Maybe he didn't understand your directions.
5. He should have been here at two.

3. Find another way Judy says . . .

1. He said, "I'll be there at two sharp." *He said he'd be here at two sharp.*
2. He said, "I know where the place is."
3. I told him, "George has an appointment that he can't be late for." (George = you)

90. He might have gotten lost.

1 ▶ Anna is looking for her keys. Listen to the conversation and check (√) the places where she hasn't looked.

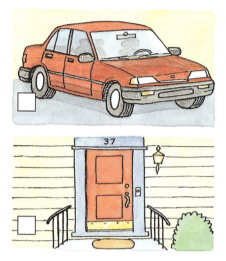

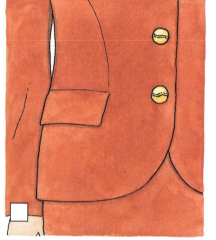

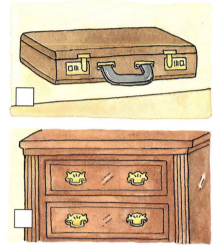

2 ▶ Listen to the conversation and practice it with a partner.
▶ Imagine you and your partner planned a business lunch for today, and four people still haven't shown up. Act out the conversations, using the information in the boxes.

A I wonder what's keeping Ed.

B He 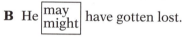 have gotten lost.

He may/might have gotten lost. = Maybe he got lost.

Some questions	Some possibilities
What's keeping Ed?	She might not have been near a phone.
Why is Carol so late?	He may have gotten lost.
Why isn't Tom here?	She may have forgotten about the appointment.
Why didn't Eva call?	He might not have understood your directions.

3 ▶ Study the frames: *May have* and *might have*

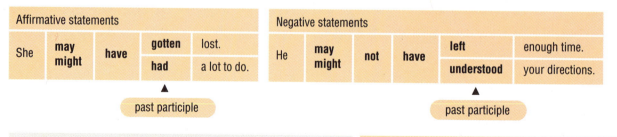

Affirmative statements

She	may might	have	gotten	lost.
			had	a lot to do.

▲ past participle

Negative statements

He	may might	not	have	left	enough time.
				understood	your directions.

▲ past participle

Use *may have* or *might have* to express possibility in the past. In these sentences, *may have* and *might have* mean about the same thing.

Notice how sentences in the past continuous are formed. Maybe she *was sleeping*. → She *may have been sleeping*.

4 ▶ Work with a partner. Look at the pictures in exercise 1 and say where Anna might have left her keys. Use *may have* or *might have*.

5 ▸ Listen to the conversation and practice it with a partner.
▸ Imagine you and your partner have been waiting for some people at a restaurant for a very long time. Act out similar conversations, using the information in the boxes.

A Do you think Ed got lost?
B Oh, I doubt it. He must not have written down the time.

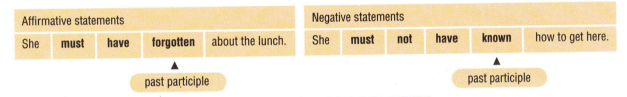

He must not have written down the time. = He probably didn't write down the time.

Some questions	Some conclusions
Do you think Ed got lost?	They must not have left themselves enough time.
Do you think Eva forgot about the meeting?	He must not have written down the time.
Do you think Carol and Tom had car trouble?	Something must have come up.

6 ▸ Study the frames: *Must have*

Affirmative statements				
She	**must**	**have**	**forgotten**	about the lunch.

▲ past participle

Negative statements					
She	**must**	**not**	**have**	**known**	how to get here.

▲ past participle

Use *must have* to state a logical conclusion about something that happened in the past.

7 ▸ Read the sentences below. Then listen to the four conversations and choose the sentence that each speaker will probably say next. Write the number of the conversation next to the correct sentence.

_____ He must have stayed late.
_____ She must not have had time to tell you.
_____ He must have taken the bus.
_____ He must have gone home.

_____ She must have taken a vacation.
_____ She must have just stepped out.
_____ She must have been at home.
_1_ He must have gotten lost.

8 ▸ Work with your classmates. Read the situations and state conclusions, using *must (not) have*. There may be more than one answer for each situation.

1. On Friday, your boss told you she might come in to the office over the weekend and catch up on her work. If she worked over the weekend, she planned to take the day off on Monday. On Monday morning, she wasn't in.
She must have worked over the weekend.

2. Yesterday you left a telephone message for a friend to call you back, but he hasn't returned your call. He's very reliable and always returns your calls promptly.

3. An hour ago, you and your friend had the same meal in a restaurant—a pasta dish in a delicious sauce. Suddenly your friend has gotten very sick, but you feel fine. Your friend is allergic to shellfish.

4. You've just arrived at your parents' home for a visit, and before you even open the front door, you can smell a delicious apple pie. Your father loves to bake.

9 ► These people are at an office party. Complete each conversation with a sentence from the box.
► Listen to check your work.

In general, use *may have* or *might have* to talk about possibilities in the past when you're not completely sure or when more than one possibility comes to mind. Use *must have* when there's a strong probability or when you're almost sure that something happened.

They may have gone to the wrong address.
You must have seen it.
Bill must have finished it.
He might not have heard about the party.
She might have been delayed.
It must have been a wrong number.

10 ► Complete the conversation, using *may (not) have*, *might (not) have*, or *must (not) have* and the correct form of the verb in parentheses.
► Practice the conversation with a partner.

A How was the surprise birthday party for Joe?
B It was fun, but he didn't look surprised at all.
A Someone _____ (tell) him about it before the party, that's for sure.
B Yeah, you're right. Who do you think told him?

A I don't know. What about Keith? He can't keep a secret. He _____ (told) him.
B Possibly. Or maybe it was Amy.
A No. She's been out of town, so it _____ (be) her.
B That's true. It _____ (be) someone else.

11 ► Work with a partner. Take turns reacting to each situation, using *may (not) have*, *might (not) have*, and *must (not) have*. Student A: You're very pessimistic and immediately think the worst. Student B: You're more optimistic.

1. Your parents are coming to visit you from out of town. They were supposed to arrive an hour ago.
   A *They must have had an accident.*
   B *They might have left the house late, or they may have gotten stuck in traffic.*

2. You applied for a job that you really want. You were supposed to find out if you got it three days ago.

3. You went out with someone two weeks ago and had a wonderful time. That person was supposed to get in touch with you again, but you haven't heard from him or her since then.

4. Your sister told you she'd be at home last night. You called her at 10:30, but there was no answer.

91. What happened?

1 ▶ **Listen to the conversation and practice it with a partner.**
   ▶ **Act out similar conversations, using the information in the boxes.**

A You were supposed to be here at noon. What happened?
B I'm sorry I'm so late. The bus broke down, so I had to walk.

Some problems
The bus broke down.
My wallet was stolen.
My car wouldn't start.
The subway stalled between stations.

Some consequences
I just had to wait it out.
I had to walk.
I had to report it to the police.
I had to take the bus.

2 ▶ **Study the frame: *Be supposed to* vs. *have to* in the past**

| She **was supposed to** | be there at noon. | ▶ She wasn't there. |
| She **had to** | | ▶ She was there. |

Use the past of *be supposed to* when an obligation was not met.
Use the past of *have to* when an obligation was met.

3 ▶ **Complete the letter with the correct form of *be supposed to* or *have to* in the past, using the verbs in parentheses.**

▶ **Write a letter of apology to someone you know. Give an excuse for not doing something you were supposed to do.**

Dear Pat,
   I can't tell you how sorry I am for all the trouble I must have caused. I know I _____ (meet) you in front of the theater at 7:30 last night, but something happened at the last minute — a pipe burst in my kitchen, and I _____ (take) care of it right then. I was able to fix it myself temporarily, but then I _____ (wait) two hours for a plumber to come! I tried to call you, but you weren't home. I know I _____ (not/do) this to you again, but it really wasn't my fault this time! Please don't be angry at me.

Chris

4 ▶ **Work with a partner.**
   Student A: Imagine you are in each of the situations in the pictures.
   Student B will remind you of what you *were supposed to* do.
   Think of a good excuse, using *had to*.
   Student B: Remind Student A of what he or she *was supposed to* do in each of the situations in the pictures.

92. Did you tell him . . . ?

1 ▶ Study the frames: Direct and reported speech

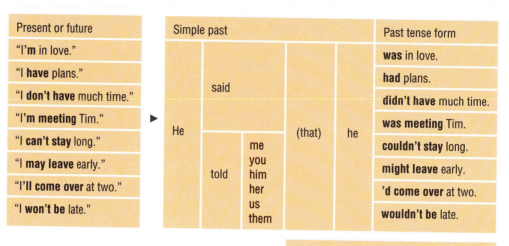

Present or future	Simple past					Past tense form
"I'**m** in love."						**was** in love.
"I **have** plans."						**had** plans.
"I **don't have** much time."	said					**didn't have** much time.
"I'**m meeting** Tim."				(that)	he	**was meeting** Tim.
"I **can't stay** long."	He		me			**couldn't stay** long.
"I **may leave** early."			you			**might leave** early.
"I'**ll come over** at two."		told	him			'**d come over** at two.
"I **won't be** late."			her			**wouldn't be** late.
			us			
			them			

Even though these forms are in the past, the meaning is still present or future.

2 ▶ Listen to the conversation and practice it with a partner.
▶ Act out similar conversations.

A I talked to Sam.
B Did you tell him (that) I had an appointment at 3:30?
A Yes, and he said (that) he'd meet us for lunch at 2:00.

George has an appointment at 3:30.

No problem. I'll meet you at 2:00.

Did you tell him . . .	He said . . .
I had an appointment at 3:30?	he'd pick you up at 5:00.
I didn't have much time to meet with him?	he'd meet us for lunch at 2:00.
I couldn't meet him before 1:30?	the meeting wouldn't take long.
9:30 was a little late to get together?	he couldn't make it any earlier.
my plane was leaving at 6:30?	that was O.K.

3 ▶ Report the following conversations, using the simple past of *say* or *tell* in your answers. Compare your answers with your classmates' answers.

1. **Nancy** I won't be home until 6:30.
   Dan I'll be home before that.
   Nancy said she wouldn't be home until 6:30.
   Dan said . . .

2. **Sue** I have to leave exactly at 5:00.
   Bill I can't stay any later than 5:00, either.
   Amy I'll stay and finish the work.

3. **Fred** I'm not planning to go to the concert because I don't have any way to get there.
   Peggy I can drive, but I won't be able to leave until 7:30.

4 ▶ Work with a partner. Think of a brief conversation you've had recently. Tell your partner the conversation as you remember it, using reported speech.

My teacher told me that my English was much better now.

Your English is much better now.

Really?

5 ▶ Read the conversations and rewrite the sentences in brackets [ ] as reported speech.
▶ Listen to check your work.
▶ Practice the conversations with a partner.

1. **A** Let's go out tonight.
   B But you said ["I want to stay home."]
   But you said that you wanted to stay home.

2. **A** I think I'll be home early tonight.
   B Really? I thought you told me ["I may be getting home late."]
   A I know, but my last two appointments got canceled.
   B Well, that's nice.

3. **A** John said ["I'll be at the Landmark Hotel, in case you need to reach me."]
   B The Landmark? I thought he said ["I'll be staying at the Intercontinental."]
   A I guess he changed his plans.

4. **A** Would you like some coffee?
   B No, thanks. I don't drink coffee anymore.
   A What? I thought you said ["I love coffee."]
   B I do, but I'm trying to cut down on caffeine.

5. **A** Mary called. She said ["I'll be a little late to the party."]
   B Oh really? She told me ["I can't make it to the party at all."]
   A Well, it looks like she changed her mind.

6. **A** I'm thinking about going to Spain for my vacation.
   B What? Last week you told me ["I'm planning to go to Hawaii."]
   A Well, I can change my mind, can't I?

6 ▶ Work with a partner. Complete each conversation with your own ideas, using reported speech. Then practice the conversations.

1. **A** It looks like it's going to rain any minute.
   B But the weather report said _____ today. It's not supposed to rain!
   A Well, you know their forecasts aren't always accurate.

2. **A** I think I'd like to spend a quiet evening at home tonight.
   B But you just said _____ .
   A I know, but I changed my mind.

3. **A** Did I tell you? I'm working at night now.
   B You are? I thought you said _____ .
   A I was, but I changed my schedule.

4. **A** I'm going to order a salad. How about you?
   B I'm going to get a hamburger.
   A What? You told me that _____ .
   B Well, I like to have one every once in a while.

7 ▶ Listen to the three messages on the Santos family's answering machine. Imagine you are a family member listening to the recordings. Write down the messages, using reported speech.

For *Maria*
WHILE YOU WERE OUT
M *Fred*
Phone No. _____
☑ TELEPHONED   ☐ PLEASE CALL
☐ WILL CALL AGAIN   ☐ RETURNED YOUR CALL
Message *He said he wanted to get together this weekend if . . .*

For *Dad*
WHILE YOU WERE OUT
M _____
Phone No. _____
☐ TELEPHONED   ☐ PLEASE CALL
☐ WILL CALL AGAIN   ☐ RETURNED YOUR CALL
Message _____

For _____
WHILE YOU WERE OUT
M _____
Phone No. _____
☐ TELEPHONED   ☐ PLEASE CALL
☐ WILL CALL AGAIN   ☐ RETURNED YOUR CALL
Message _____

93. As it turns out . . .

That evening Lou has some new surprises.

1. Listen in

Lou gets a phone call from Carol Thomas. Read the questions below. Then listen to the phone conversation and answer the questions.

1. Why wasn't Carol able to get hold of Lou?
2. What did Lou forget to do?

2

(Lou goes to answer his door.)

Lou Kate! I've been worried sick. . . .

Kate I've been trying to call you since Sunday night, but there was no answer.

Lou My phone was out of order. I didn't realize it until this morning.

Kate So, is anything new?

Lou Quite a bit, in fact! The Kims' house was broken into, and the Riveras' mask was missing. . . .

Kate Oh, no, Lou, how awful!

Lou Well, as it turns out, the Riveras' niece took the mask. She was playing with it and forgot to tell them.

Kate With me disappearing, they must have wondered if I'd taken it. Anyway, I really do owe you an explanation.

Lou I'm dying of curiosity.

Kate Listen, I apologize, Lou. The truth is that I couldn't work because I had an audition in New York. I thought it might be bad luck to talk about it beforehand. I was supposed to be through by Saturday. Anyway, the good news is that I'm going to be in a Broadway show!

Lou That's great! *(Quietly)* I guess that means I'm without a partner, then. But I wish you the best of luck.

Kate Thanks, Lou. This is something I've always wanted. I've never told you before, but I'm really a dancer.

Lou I still can't get over it. These past few weeks have been full of surprises.

Kate Remember when I told you that we moved a lot when I was young? Maybe now you can guess why.

Lou One of your parents was a dancer?

Kate My mother was.

Lou And I bet your father was a cabinetmaker.

Kate *(Smiling)* How did you ever guess?

Lou Gee, Kate. I'm going to miss you.

Kate Well, you know, Lou, New York is only a plane ride away.

3. Figure it out

Check (√) the sentences that are stated or implied in the conversation.

1. _____ Kate tried to get hold of Lou on Sunday.
2. _____ Kate knew about the burglary at the Kims' house.
3. _____ Kate tried out for the most important dancing part in a Broadway show.
4. _____ Kate didn't tell Lou about her audition because she was afraid he'd fire her.
5. _____ Kate thought she'd be back in time for work on Monday.
6. _____ Kate must have learned cabinetwork from her father.
7. _____ Kate and Lou don't want to say good-bye.

94. Your turn

Read the puzzles below. Then work in groups to figure out the answers. When you are discussing possibilities, use the expressions *may (not) have, might (not) have,* and *must (not) have.* You may look up the answers to this exercise on page 165.

The Haircut

A new man in town needed a haircut. He learned that there were only two barbers in town. He went to the first barber's shop and saw that it was very dirty, with hair all over the floor. In fact, the barber himself needed a haircut and a shave. Then he went to the second barber's shop. It was neat and clean, and the barber himself was as neat as his shop. He didn't need a shave, and he had a good haircut. The man decided to have the first barber cut his hair. Why?

Which Door?

A king locked a man in a room with two other men. The room had two doors, one to freedom and the other to prison. The captive had to choose one of the doors. The captive was told that both men knew which door led to freedom. He was allowed to ask each of the two men one question. He knew that one of the men always lied and the other always told the truth, but he didn't know which man was the liar. The captive went free. What questions did he ask?

Families

A man pointed to a family photograph and said to his son: "Brothers and sisters I have none, but that man's father is my father's son." Who was the man pointing to?

🔲 How to say it

Practice the phrases. Then practice the conversation.

must have [mɨ́stəv]   should have [ʃʊ́dəv]

might have [máɪtəv]   may have [méəv]

A Linda was supposed to be here an hour ago. She must have left her house late.

B She might have had trouble with her car.

A She should have called us, then.

B But she might not have our phone number. I may have forgotten to give it to her.

CHRONIC LATENESS
Learning to Leave It Behind
by DIANE COLE

Everyone is late sometimes. But do you know anyone who is always late? Do you think there's a reason why some people are chronically late? Read the article to find out.

At the theater, she disrupts the first act as she climbs over your knees toward her seat. When your doorbell rings on a Saturday night, long after your other guests have begun eating, you know he has arrived for dinner. At work, you don't expect her at your 9:00 A.M. meeting.

They are the latecomers, and it doesn't matter if they wear a watch or use an alarm clock. Lateness is their way of life.

Chronic lateness has spoiled friendships, and it's a habit that has caused people to lose their jobs. Why, then, are so many people late?

"Not arriving on time can be a form of avoidance," says Dr. Richard Kravitz, a psychiatrist at Yale–New Haven Medical Center in Connecticut. "You're late for a party, maybe, or coming home from work, because you don't want to be where you're supposed to be."

Other reasons for chronic lateness are more complex. Dr. Kravitz suggests that some latecomers may have masochistic tendencies. They know that their lateness will cause anger, and this serves their deep need to be punished. Alternatively, some latecomers may have a sadistic motive. For them, forcing someone to wait is a way of expressing anger or resentment.

Dr. Herbert Fensterheim, a psychologist at New York Cornell Medical Center, agrees that lateness can be used as a weapon with which to strike out at someone. However, he adds that for some people lateness is nothing more than a habit learned in childhood from a parent or an older brother or sister who also ran late. For others, lateness is a result of an inability to judge time. There are also those who are so easily distracted that they simply "lose track" of time, while others never learn to estimate or leave the time they need to keep on schedule.

As for those of us who wait, we can set limits as to how long we will stay before leaving. When appropriate, we can make our anger known. And though it is true that being prompt can be as compulsive as being late, Shakespeare advised this: "Better three hours too soon than a minute too late."

**1. Read the article.
Then choose *a*, *b*, or *c*.**

1. The main purpose of the first paragraph is to
   a. give reasons.
   b. describe events.
   c. give an opinion.

2. The main purpose of the fourth and fifth paragraphs is to
   a. give reasons.
   b. describe events.
   c. give sympathy.

3. The main purpose of the sixth paragraph is to
   a. give alternative reasons.
   b. disagree with someone.
   c. show that being late is wrong.

4. A chronic latecomer is someone who
   a. always loses his or her job.
   b. is sorry he or she is late.
   c. is almost always late.

5. A masochistic person is someone who
   a. likes to hurt people.
   b. wants to be punished.
   c. is angry.

**2. Which of these points does the article make?
Say *True* or *False*.**

1. Some people are late because they don't want to be where they are supposed to be going.

2. Some people are late because they are angry at the person they are supposed to meet.

3. All latecomers have serious psychological problems.

4. Some people learn to be late when they are children.

Review of units 12-14

1 ▶ Rewrite the conversation between two friends, Karen and Peter, using the expressions in parentheses.
▶ Practice the conversation with a partner.

Karen Isn't Mary coming to the movies with us? (I thought . . .) *I thought Mary was coming to the movies with us.*

Peter She has too much work to do. (She said . . .)

Karen Is she planning to have dinner with us? (Do you know . . . ?)

Peter She will if she finishes her work. (She told me . . .)

Karen Maybe I should call her. (I wonder . . .) She may not know where the restaurant is. (What if . . . ?)

Peter That's a good idea. By the way, have you made a reservation at the restaurant?

Karen We don't need one, do we? (I didn't think. . .) In fact, I completely forgot about it.

Peter Maybe we should call. Will they take us without one? (I don't think . . .)

Karen O.K. I'll call the restaurant from the movie theater. I'm sorry I didn't call them sooner. (I should . . .)

2 ▶ Read the sentences and then listen to Peter and Karen's conversation. Who said each sentence? Write *P* for Peter and *K* for Karen.

____ I'm planning to take a vacation.
____ I'm thinking about Mexico City.
____ I love Mexico.
____ Mexico City is a really exciting place.
____ If I go, it'll be my first trip there.
____ There are so many things to see and do.
____ I'm going to see a travel agent tomorrow.
____ I hope I can get a good package deal.

▶ Work with a partner. Talk about Peter and Karen's conversation, using reported speech.

Karen said she was planning to take a vacation. She said . . .

3A ▶ Student A follows the instructions below.
▶ Student B follows the instructions on page 158.

Student A You'd like to take a trip and you've been considering Mexico City. Call Student B, who's a travel agent. Ask the questions in the box, beginning each one with *Could you tell me . . . ?, Do you know . . . ?,* or *Do you have any idea . . . ?*

Think of another place you would like to visit.
Ask Student B the same questions and any others you might have about that place.

How much are the tickets?
Are there less expensive airfares?
How often are there flights?
Will I have to change planes?
What's the weather like in . . . ?
Do I need a passport or a visa?
Are there package deals that include hotels, meals, and sightseeing?
Does anyone speak . . . in . . . ?

3B ▸ Student B follows the instructions below.
▸ Student A follows the instructions on page 157.

Student B Imagine you are a travel agent, and Student A calls you for information. Answer his or her questions, using the information on the travel agent's card and your own knowledge.

Student A will ask you questions about another place that he or she might like to visit. Answer Student A's questions. Use your imagination and your knowledge of the place your partner wants to visit.

Travel Agent's Pick
MEXICO CITY
Airfare: regularly $999 round-trip; supersaver $519 with a Saturday night stayover
Flights: 1 nonstop daily, 2 nonstops Fridays (in both directions)
Air/land package: 4 nights for 2 people including airfare, accommodations, meals, and bus tours: $879 per person + tax
Language: Spanish; English widely spoken
Weather: Mild climate in high altitude; almost no rain October–April. Winters can be cool.
Passport required, except for North Americans

4 ▸ Complete the conversations, using *might have*, *may have*, *must have*, or *should have* and the correct form of the verb in parentheses.

1. **A** Last night I was awakened by a loud crash in the kitchen.
   B You <u>must have been</u> (be) scared to death.
   A I was. At first, I thought it _____ (be) a burglar, but I wasn't sure. Then I heard this voice saying, "Meow, meow," and there was no doubt.
   B It _____ (be) the cat!
   A That's exactly what it was.

2. **A** Guess what? My sister showed up last night for a surprise visit!
   B She did? Your family _____ (be) really happy.
   A We sure were. But my mother kept telling her, "You _____ (tell) us you were coming!"
   B Doesn't your mother like surprises?
   A I guess she thought she _____ (bake) a cake.

3. **A** I wonder what happened to Tim and Sue? It's awfully late.
   B Well, they _____ (get) stuck in traffic. It's very possible on a Friday afternoon. Or they _____ (not/leave) home when they planned to.
   A That's true. Oh, wait, Sue said they might stop for lunch on the way. That's what they _____ (do).
   B I bet you're right.

4. **A** I just had a fight with Gary on the telephone. He hung up before I could even apologize.
   B He _____ (be) really angry.
   A He sure was. I _____ (not/call) him. I knew he was in a bad mood.

5 ▸ Two people are discussing their plans for the day. Put the lines of the conversation in order.
▸ Practice the conversation with a partner.

____ Oh, no. I'm too tired to go running.
____ It might. I guess we don't have to go out at all.
____ But isn't it supposed to rain?
____ I *do* want to exercise more, but I haven't got enough energy to go running right now.
____ Well, we don't have to go running. How about a walk instead?
_8_ Good. I'd rather watch the Olympic games on TV, anyway.
____ Let's go running in the park.
____ I thought you wanted to get more exercise.

6
- ▶ Work with a partner. Find out some interesting things about your partner by asking the questions in the box and your own questions. Take turns asking and answering.
- ▶ If any of your partner's answers surprise you, respond by saying *I didn't know . . . , I didn't think . . . , I had no idea . . .* , or *I thought . . .*

I speak Mandarin Chinese fluently.
I didn't know you could speak Mandarin.

Some questions

How many languages do you speak?
 (Which ones?)
How many different countries have you been to?
 (Which ones?)
Where were you born?
Where did you grow up?
Do you play any sports? (Which ones?)
Do you like to cook? (Which dishes?)
Can you sing?
Do you have any interesting hobbies?
 (What are they?)

7
- ▶ Work with your classmates. Take turns reporting interesting information that you discovered in exercise 6. Express surprise whenever appropriate.

Did you know that Claudia could ride wild horses?
Really? I didn't know you could ride, Claudia.

8
- ▶ Work in groups of three. Imagine you and your two classmates need to arrange a lunch meeting tomorrow.

Student A First find out if Student B is free for lunch tomorrow. Suggest the Mouthful Restaurant. Then talk to Student C about the time and place. After you've made arrangements with Student C, report the conversation to Student B. (*He/She said that . . .*)

Student B Student A will ask you about lunch plans for tomorrow. You can get together tomorrow for lunch, but you'll have to leave the restaurant by 2:00 P.M. Any restaurant is O.K. with you. Then, after Student A makes plans with Student C, ask Student A about his or her conversation. (*Did you tell him/her that . . . ?*)

Student C You're free for lunch any time tomorrow. You've been to the Mouthful Restaurant many times. Make plans with Student A.

- ▶ Change roles until everyone has played each part. When you change roles, also change some of the information, using your own ideas.

9
- ▶ Listen to the first part of each conversation and choose the best response.

1. a. I thought we were going to a movie.
   b. I'm too tired to go out.

2. a. Yes, there's one right on the corner.
   b. I doubt it.

3. a. I'm Polish.
   b. I *am* Polish.

4. a. I can't think of one.
   b. Most likely.

5. a. But I had to be back at work today.
   b. But I'm not supposed to be back at work today.

6. a. He may not have understood the directions.
   b. He may have understood the directions.

7. a. I'm sorry. I had to be home an hour ago.
   b. I'm sorry. I should have called.

8. a. I'm too full to eat another bite.
   b. No, I'm too hungry.

9. a. Doesn't he like it?
   b. I'm sure he'll like it.

10. a. She should have forgotten.
    b. She must have forgotten.

10 ► Read the article. Then complete the following statements.

1. Oscar Wilde said that the English _had everything in common with the Americans except language_.
2. A British literary critic once said that he _____ .
3. H.L. Mencken thought that the English spoken in the United States _____ .
4. _____ would write the sentence "My favourite theatre is the Savoy."
5. If a British woman needed help in a clothing store, she'd talk to _____ .

11 ► How would these conversations be different if Americans, not British people, were speaking? Change the underlined parts of the sentences to their American equivalents.
► Practice the conversations.

1. **A** Look at that <u>queue</u>! We should have <u>booked a table</u>. _Look at that line! We should have made a reservation._
   B Why don't we try that little restaurant <u>in</u> Dunster Street?

2. **A** Excuse me—which way is the <u>gents</u>?
   B Straight <u>on</u>.

3. **A** I'm going <u>out to the shops</u> now.
   B If you're going past the <u>chemist's</u>, can you get me some aspirin?
   A <u>What sort</u>?
   B <u>Any'll do</u> . Oh, and would you mind <u>posting</u> this letter for me, if it's not too much trouble?
   A Not at all.

4. **A** I'm going to the <u>pictures</u>. <u>Do you fancy coming</u> along? There's a good western <u>on</u>.
   B <u>I'm not that keen on westerns</u>. But thanks for inviting me.

5. **A** (_Phone rings_) <u>That'll be</u> Bob. Will you get it, Helen, and tell him I'll ring back in ten minutes?
   B O.K.
   C May I speak to Jane, please?
   B Is <u>that</u> Bob?
   C Yes.
   B Jane's <u>having</u> a shower. Can she <u>ring</u> you back in ten minutes?
   C Fine.

English on Both Sides of the Atlantic

The following sign once appeared, it is said, in a Paris shop window: ENGLISH SPOKEN—AMERICAN UNDERSTOOD.

The French aren't the only ones who have made humorous references to the differences between these two "languages." Oscar Wilde, the Irish dramatist, commented: "The English have really everything in common with the Americans, except of course language." A British literary critic spoke of being "bilingual in the two branches of English."

Is the English spoken in the United States a different language from the English spoken in Great Britain? H.L. Mencken, an American who shortly after World War I published his book _The American Language_, evidently thought so. But no serious modern linguist holds this opinion. The grammatical structure is for the most part the same. There are, of course, many differences in pronunciation and some in spelling. The British write _colour_; Americans write _color_. The British write _theatre_; Americans write _theater_. And there are quite a number of differences in vocabulary as well. Norman W. Schur, in _British Self-Taught with Comments in American_, points out that a British woman looking in a store window would probably say, "I'd like to go into that shop and look at that frock," while her friend from the United States would more likely say, "I'd like to go into that store and look at that dress." The British woman might have said "dress," but would not have said "store." The woman from the United States might have said "shop," but would never have said "frock." And the person who waited on them would be a "salesperson" in the United States, but a "shop assistant" in Britain.

The similarities between British and American English are far greater than the differences. And with modern communications—the British watching telly and going to the cinema on one side of the Atlantic and Americans watching TV and going to the movies on the other—these two dialects of English are moving closer together all the time.

Look at the queue!

Look at that line!

VOCABULARY LIST

This list includes both productive and receptive words introduced in Student Book 4. Productive words are those which students use actively in interaction exercises. Receptive words are those which appear only in opening conversations, comprehension dialogues, readings, and instructions, and which students need only understand. The following abbreviations are used to identify words: V = verb, N = noun, ADJ = adjective, PREP = preposition, CONJ = conjunction, R = receptive. Page numbers indicate the first appearance of a word.

A a couple of 3
accessory 143 R
accidental 100 R
abandon (V) 10 R
able 32
absence 10 R
accidentally 96
accommodation(s) 129
accurate 153
accustomed (grow accustomed) 13 R
acquainted (ADJ) 89 R
actual 64
add up 109 R
advance (ADJ) 52 R
advanced (ADJ) 10 R
advancing (ADJ) 39 R
advantage 74
advice 103
advise (V) 156 R
affect (V) 110 R
affection 109 R
age (in ages) 112
agree (V) 140
ahead (go ahead) 83
air conditioner 85
aircraft 80
airfare 129
airplane 4
ajar 42
alert 110 R
allergic 95
along with 10 R
alongside 10 R
alternatively 156 R
American-born 23
amusing (ADJ) 143 R
analysis 90 R
anger 156 R
anguish 29 R
anniversary 89 R
announcer 72
annoyed (ADJ) 82
anticipate (V) 110 R
anticipation 11 R
anxiety 76 R
anyhow 118
anyplace 34 R
anywhere 80
apart (take apart) 90 R
apologize 35
appeal (V) 40 R
appliance (home appliance) 63
appreciation (art appreciation) 90 R
approach (V) 76 R
appropriately 84 R
aptitude 90 R
argue (V) 75
argument 103
army 39 R
arrangement 21 R
artistic 56 R
as long as 118
as usual 107 R
aspect 20 R
assault 30 R

astronomy 90 R
at ease 90 R
athlete 40 R
atlas 37
attend (V) 122
attic 92
attractively 135 R
audition 154
autobiography 29
automobile 9
avoidance 156 R
awake 95
awaken (V) 158

B baby-sit (V) 22
backwards 6 R
bake (V) 131
balanced (ADJ) 109
ball 73
barber 123
basement 63
be able to 32
be about to 84 R
be rid of 20 R
be used to 13
bear (animal) 70
beauty 136
beforehand 154
behalf (on behalf of) 89 R
being (N) 76 R
beneficial 40 R
benefit (of the doubt) 132
beside (PREP) 118
bet (V) 154
bill (to be paid) 84 R
biography 90 R
bite (a bite to eat) 146
bite off (V) 110 R
blackboard 77
bleach 97
blow (up) (V) 103
boarding pass 80
boil (V) 131
boiling (ADJ) 96 R
bold 30 R
bookcase 64
bookend 143 R
boot 63
bother (V) 58
bracelet 63
break (something) up 3
break down (into) 40 R
break down (V) 147
break into 42
break-in 42
briefly 114 R
bright and early 88
bring (someone) up 46
bring (something) in for 42 R
browse 46 R
bruise (V) 96
bump (into) (V) 96
burglar 132
burglarize (V) 42
burglary 132
burn (N) 100 R
burner (on a stove) 99
burst (V) 151 R

butter 131
butterfly 139
by (with agent) 23

C cabinetmaker 18
café 126
cabinetmaking 38 R
cabinetwork 28
caffeine 153
call-in 107 R
calm down (V) 113
calming (ADJ) 42 R
canal 10 R
cancel (V) 73
candlelight 8
capable (of) 120 R
capital (city) 37
captive 155 R
capture (V) 39 R
carefully 141
carpenter 43 R
carpet 100 R
case (passport case) 143 R
catalogue 62
catch fire 70
cathedral 134 R
cattle 53
cave 25
CD player 137
celebrity 66 R
ceremonial 55
chain 144 R
chance (N) (take a chance) 54
change (N) (of plans, etc.) 82
change one's mind 153
character 23
charity 51
check-in/checkout (time) 129
checkered (ADJ) 39 R
chew (V) 110 R
chewing gum 117
childhood 49
childish 5 R
childproof 100 R
chilly 85
choice 79
chop (up) (V) 96
chore 121
chronic 96
civilization 30 R
claim (V) 66 R
classical 137
classified (ads) 22
clean (ADJ) 5
clean out (V) 92
clean up (V) 86
clip (tie clip) 143 R
clock 143 R
closely 30 R
clothing 53
clown (N) 6 R
clue 132
clutter 100 R
coat (V) 59 R
code (country code) 37
collect (V) 139
comb (N) 144 R
come out as 3

come over one 103
come to mind 150 R
come true 30 R
come up (= happen) 88
command (V) 90 R
communicate (V) 117 R
competent 19 R
complex 156 R
complimentary 129
compose (V) 24
composition 77
compulsive 156 R
concentrate (V) 85
concentration 90 R
concern (N) (= worry) 88
concern (V) 110 R
concerned (ADJ) 88 R
conclusion (jump to a conclusion) 132
confusion 64
conquer (V) 10 R
conquest 10 R
considerate 121
considerate 65 R
consist of (V) 10 R
consistent 40 R
constructive 110 R
consume (V) 109 R
consumer 112
container 100 R
content (N) 21 R
contest (N) 115
continue (V) 50
contribution 51
cooperate (V) 42
cooperative 110 R
cord (extension cord) 99
cordless (telephone) 63
cosmetics 63
costume jewelry 42
cough (V) 104
counsel (V) (= advise) 110 R
courage 134 R
cow 41 R
coworker 84
craft (= handicraft) 55
crash (N) (= loud noise) 158
credit (V) 80
crime 38
criminal 38 R
crop 10 R
cry (V) 106
curb 71 R
curiosity 154
currency 128
cut away 56 R

D damage (N and V) 100 R
dancer 38
darling 144 R
day-care 21 R
day-to-day 109 R
deadline 110 R
deal (N) 157
death (scare to death) 68
degree (from a university) 2
delay (V) 116
delegate (V) 110 R

161

lateness 156 R
lay off 22
lazy 41 R
lead to (V) 155 R
leading (ADJ) 100 R
leaf (raking leaves) 40 R
lean (V) 99
leap (up) (V) 144 R
length 9 R
lesson 113
let (someone) down 82
let alone (= not to mention)
    126
let loose 30 R
level 40 R
Lg. (= large) 139 R
liar 155 R
liberty 80 R
librarian 90 R
licensed (ADJ) 21 R
lick (V) 134 R
lie (V) (= tell an untruth) 155 R
likely 127
limit (N) 156 R
limit (V) 91 R
limited (ADJ) 11
lineup 5 R
literature 72
lobby 80
logical 146
look (something) over 135 R
look (something) up 32
look after 23 R
look around 18
lose one's balance 96
lose one's temper 103
lose track of 156 R
loudly 68
lovely 136
lower (ADJ) 96

M magic 135 R
mail (V) 58
mailbox 88
main 23
majority 20 R
make sense 96
make up (= become friendly
    again) 74
manufacture (V) 53
mask 54
master's degree 2
match (N) (= contest) 39 R
material 118
mattress 91 R
mature 22
may have 148
Med. (= medium) 139 R
meditation 110 R
mental 76 R
might have 146
mighty 144 R
mild 158 R
millionaire 27
mind (V) (= take care of) 21 R
minimize 100 R
minority 21 R
missing (ADJ) 32
mistaken (ADJ) 125 R
misuse (N) 100 R
model (person) 66 R
motive 156 R
motto 40 R
mountain 9
mounted (ADJ) 143 R
mouthful 159 R
muscle 70
museum piece 54

must have 146
mysterious 132

N nag (V) 92
nail (polish) 63
nagging (ADJ) 96
nearly 150
neat 155 R
necessarily 90 R
neighboring (ADJ) 10 R
nervously 136 R
net 39 R
network 66 R
newlywed 105 R
no-risk 117
none of (someone's)
    business 103
nonfiction 29
nonhuman 30 R
nursing (N) 47
nut 143 R

O object (= purpose)
    (N) 39 R
observe (V) 125 R
objective 30 R
occasional 76 R
ocean 9
offer (V) 43
offhand 26
Olympic games 158
on (someone's) back 82
on and off 38
on arrival 129
on the line 82
on top of 64
on-again-off-again 96
once in a while 22
one-of-a-kind 56 R
ongoing (ADJ) 114 R
onto 71 R
opener (letter opener) 143 R
opening (N) 36
openly 109 R
opponent 39 R
option 21 R
organize (V) 32 R
out (=not possible, not
    acceptable) 32
out of order 154
out of place 64
out of the way 57
out of town 69
outdoor (ADJ) 82
outlet (electrical outlet) 99
oven 131
over nothing 103
overcoat 144 R
overhear (V) 18
overloaded (ADJ) 100 R
overseas 19 R
overwhelming (ADJ)
overwork (N) 103 R

P pace (N) 103
painter 56 R
pace (V) 146
package tour/trip 129
page 117
painful 91 R
painting (N) 25
pan 8
paper (for school) 8
paperwork 110 R
parallel park (V) 118
participate (V) 109 R
partner 154
pass out (V) 76 R

passion 42 R
patient (N) 47
pattern 21 R
payment 80
peel (N) (banana peel) 96
pelvis 91 R
peppermint 135 R
per (PREP) 158 R
percent 136
perfume 63
period (of time) 132
permit (N) 95
permit (V) 80
person 9
philosophical 30 R
phonograph 24
photocopy 60
photography 139
pick (N) 158
pick (pockets) (V) 38
pick out (= select) (V) 136
pineapple 53
place (N) 9
place (V) 56 R
plan (N and V) 82
play (a trick, tricks) 76 R
plug (N and V) 99
point (N) 10 R
poison/poisoning 100 R
polish (shoe polish) 61
politeness 20 R
politician 30 R
politics 29 R
pool (swimming pool) 101 R
possibly 32
postpone (V) 110 R
posture 91 R
pour (V) 70
powdered (ADJ) 131 R
practically 38
practice (N) 37
practiced (ADJ) 144 R
precaution 100 R
precise 42
preparation 20 R
prescription 58
presentation 124 R
preserve 29 R
pressured (ADJ) 101 R
pride 144 R
principal 39 R
print (N) (of a drawing,
    painting, etc.) 46
printing (N) 47
prison 52 R
probability 148 R
process (N) 56 R
produce (V) 53
product 53
professional 54
progress (N) 11 R
prohibition 91 R
project (N) 110 R
promise (V) 88
promote (V) 25
prompt (ADJ) 156 R
promptly 149
pronunciation 11
propose (V) 110 R
provider 21 R
publication 90 R
pull (N) 66 R
pull (something) down 144 R
pull a muscle 96
pull up 118
punish (V) 119
purchase (V) 66 R

pure 139 R
purse 38
pursue (V) 90 R
put (something) off
    (= postpone) 85
put (two and two together) 108
put in touch with 28

Q quick 117
quietly 66 R
quotation 20 R

R race (V) 71 R
racket (= loud
    noise) 110 R
raincoat 63
raise (V) 53
range (from) (V) 110 R
range (mountain range) 9
rapidly 144 R
rate (N) 129
rate (V) 40 R
reach (V) 153
react (V) 6 R
real-life 64
realize (V) 142
rearrange 79 R
reason 98
receive (V) 80
redo (V) 64
reduce (V) 40 R
refill (V) 79
regret (N) 135 R
regret (V) 141 R
rehearsal 37
relate to 64
relaxation 91 R
reliable 149
rep. (= representative) 122 R
repair (N) 123
repair (V) 79
repetitive 114 R
report (V) 151
representative 145 R
requirement 26 R
research (N) 51
resentment 156 R
reservation (Indian
    reservation) 55
residential 10 R
resource 29 R
restate (V) 87 R
restrict (V) 109 R
result (in) (V) 100 R
resume (V) 45 R
retailer 66 R
retell (V) 50 R
reunion 35
revelation 30 R
revolution 27
rewarding (ADJ) 110 R
rich 117
rid of (be rid of) 20 R
rights 27
ripple (V) 144 R
rite 10 R
river 9
routine 8
royal 7
rude 71
rug 55
ruin (V) 82
run (N) 131

S safety 100 R
salesperson 44
salty 73
satisfaction 117

ANSWERS

Your turn, page 9

1. The highest waterfall in the world is Angel Falls in *Venezuela*. It is 3,212 feet (979 meters) high.
2. The longest wall in the world is the Great Wall of *China*. It is over 2,000 miles (1,250 kilometers) long.
3. The longest street in the world is Yonge Street, which starts in Toronto, *Canada*. It is over 1,100 miles (687 kilometers) long.
4. The most popular country for tourists is *France*, which sometimes receives over 50 million visitors a year.
5. The longest rivers in the world are *the Nile* and *the Amazon*, both approximately 4,000 miles (2,500 kilometers) long.
6. The largest ocean in the world is *the Pacific*, which covers an area of approximately 64,000,000 square miles (16,575,936,000 hectares).
7. The place with the densest automobile traffic in the world is *Hong Kong*, with about 4.5 yards (4.113 meters) per vehicle on driveable roads.
8. The city with the largest taxi fleet is *Mexico City*, with over 60,000 taxis.
9. The coldest place in the world is in *Antarctica*, with an annual mean temperature of about -72°F (58°C).
10. The longest mountain range in the world is *the Andes*, in South America. It is approximately 4,700 miles (2,937 kilometers) long.

Exercise 2, page 24

War and Peace was written by Tolstoy.
The telephone was invented by Bell.
The *Mona Lisa* was painted by da Vinci.
Madame Butterfly was composed by Puccini.
The phonograph was invented by Edison.

Your turn, page 55

a. jewelry (silver/Mexico)
b. ceremonial mask (wood/Africa)
c. rug (wool/Navajo Indian reservation, Southwestern U.S.A.)
d. wine glass (glass/Venice, Italy)
e. aboriginal bark painting (bark/Australia)

Exercise 6, page 105

Dear Newlywed,
If I were you, I'd talk to your husband without delay. Both of you have been coming home from work with different expectations. That, by itself, can lead to problems. You're right to avoid confrontation: I'd approach him diplomatically, but firmly, and point out the chores that need to be done in the house. I'd ask him which ones he'd prefer to do. If he says 'None' then I'd simply stop doing half of the household chores. Most people are willing to negotiate after they've been wearing dirty socks for two weeks! —ANDY

Your turn, page 133

top left: Venice, Italy
middle left: Kyoto, Japan
bottom left: Bangkok, Thailand
top right: Easter Island
middle right: Moscow, Russia
bottom right: Istanbul, Turkey

Lesson 88, page 144

The end of the story "The Gift" is:
"Dell," said Jim, "let's put our Christmas presents away and keep them awhile. They're too nice to use just at present. I sold the watch to buy the combs."

Your turn, page 155

The Haircut

Because there were only two barbers in town, the second barber, whose hair was neatly cut, must have gone to the first one. Therefore, the man knew that the first barber gave good haircuts. The second barber's shop might have benn very clean because he had no customers.

Which Door?

Question 1: Do both doors go to freedom?
The captive knows that the answer to this question is no. Therefore, if one of the men answers yes, the captive will know he is the liar.
Question 2: Which door goes to freedom?
Now that the captive knows which man is the liar, he will know whether the answer is correct.

Families

The man was pointing to himself.

A C K N O W L E D G M E N T S

ILLUSTRATIONS: Storyline illustrations by Anna Veltfort: pages 2, 3, 8, 18, 28, 38, 54, 64, 74, 88, 98, 108, 118, 132, 142, 154, and 159; pages 16, 48 (top), 49 (bottom), 67, 68, 69, 96, 104, 105, 122, and 157 by Anne Burgess; pages 12, 13, 65, 72, 82, 83, 129, 138, 148 (bottom), and 149 by Hugh Harrison; pages 5, 11, 41, 71, 75, 84, 97, 102, 103, 119, 140, 145, 146, 147, and 152 by Randy Jones; pages 4, 32, 33, 39, 40, 48 (bottom), 49 (top), 61, 78 (middle), 79 (bottom), 85, 94, 106, 107, 117 (bottom), 121, 136, 137, 141, 151, and 160 by V. Gene Myers; pages 6, 24, 36, 45 (bottom left), 51, 63, 70, 77 (middle), 92, 93, 130, 131, 155, and 158 by Charles Peale; pages 26, 44, 45 (bottom right), 46, 47, 81, 126, and 127 by Janet Pietrobono; pages 17, 50, 57, 58, 59, 77 (bottom), 78 (top and bottom), 79 (middle), 117 (top), 125, 128, and 150 by Bot Roda; pages 15, 34, 35, 60, 79, 86, 114, 115, and 148 (top) by Arnie Ten.

PHOTOS: Pages 1, 7 (third), 14 (fourth), 25 (bottom left), 43 (top left and bottom left), 52 (middle), 56, 133 (top right) by Superstock; pages 4 (top) by Four by Five; page 4 (bottom) by Travelpix/FPG International; page 7 (first) by Robert Huntsinger/Stock Market; page 7 (second) by Karen Leeds/Stock Market; page 7 (fourth) by Photoworld/FPG International; page 9 (top) by Navaswan/FPG International; page 9 (middle) by John Robert/Stock Market; page 9 (bottom) by Henry Fichner/Photo Graphics; page 10 by Olaf Soot/Tony Stone Images; page 12 by Lehtikuva Oy; page 13 by Bellavia/Rea/SABA/R.É.A.; page 14 (first) by Karl Weatherly/Tony Stone Images; page 14 (second) by Tim Brown/Tony Stone Images; page 14 (third) by Ron Chapple/FPG International; pages 20, 22, 23, 89, 99, 111, 112, and 113 by Frank Labua; page 21 by Ed Bock/Stock Market; page 25 (top left) by David Sutherland/Tony Stone Images; page 25 (bottom right) by Lee Kuhn/FPG International; page 25 (top right), 146 by The Telegraph Colour Library FPG International; pages 27 and 29 by Tim Davis; page 42 (top right) by Stock Boston; page 42 (middle left) by National Archives; page 42 (middle right) by Barbara Alper/Stock Boston; page 42 (top left), 52 (left), and 106 (left) by Rhoda Sidney; page 42 (bottom left) by Bob Daemmrich/Stock Boston; page 42 (bottom right) by Spenser Grant/Stock Boston; page 43 (bottom middle) by Grant Faint/The Image Bank; page 43 (bottom middle) by Gary Bistram/The Image Bank; page 43 by (right) Chris Michaels/FPG International; page 45 by Carol Graham/FPG International; page 50 (top right) by Michael Tcherevkoff/The Image Bank; page 50 (bottom right) by Paul Barton/Stock Market; page 50 (left), 143 (first) by David de Lossy/The Image Bank; page 52 (right) by Garrett Kalleberg; page 55 (top right) by Pamela Dewey/National Museum of the American Indian; page 55 (top left) by Karen Furth/National Museum of the American Indian; page 55 (middle right) by Doria Steedman/Stock Market; page 55 (bottom left) by Penny Tweedle/Tony Stone Images; page 55 (bottom right) by The Corning Museum of Glass; page 62 by Federal Reserve; page 76 by Photofest; page 80 by Donald Dietz/Stock Boston; page 91 by Fredryka Himmelbrand/FPG International; page 94 by Eberhard E. Otto/FPG International; page 101 by Art Stieh/Photo Researchers; page 106 (right) by The Image Work; page 110 by Douglas Bowles/The Image Bank; page 123 (top) by Stephen McBrady/Photoedit; page 123 (middle) by Jan Lukas/Photo Researchers; page 123 by Mimi Forsyth/Monkmeyer Press; page 130 by Brett Froomer/The Image Bank; page 133 (top and bottom left) by FPG International; page 133 (middle left) by Hugh Sitton/Superstock; pages 133 (middle right) by Luis Villota/Stock Market; page 133 (bottom right) by Hugh Sitton/Tony Stone Images; page 143 (second) by Elaine Sulle/The Image Bank; page 143 (third) by Spencer Grant/Monkmeyer Press; page 143 (fourth) by Bard Martin/The Image Bank.

REALIA: Pages 5, 10, 15, 19, 20, 21, 26, 30, 31, 35, 36, 37, 40, 42, 43, 52, 53, 56, 66, 76, 77, 80, 89, 90, 91, 95, 97, 100, 101, 104, 106 (top), 109, 110, 120, 122, 123, 124 (top), 125, 131, 134, 135, 139, 143, 144, 153, 156 and 158 by Siren Design; pages 1, 16, 63, 86, 87, 105, 106 (bottom), 107, and 160 by Anna Veltfort; pages 62, 124 (bottom), 129, 130, 140, and 151 by Ken Liao.

PERMISSIONS: Page 27: Cover reprinted by permission of the Putnam Publishing Group from *The Joy Luck Club* by Amy Tan. ©1989 by Amy Tan; page 27: Cover from *The Grapes of Wrath* by John Steinbeck. ©1967 by John Steinbeck. Used by permission of Viking Penguin, a division of Penguin Books USA Inc.; page 27: Jacket illustration and flap copy from *The Death of Artemio Cruz* by Carlos Fuentes, in a new translation by Alfred MacAdam. Jacket design ©1991 by Drenntel Doyle Partners. Jacket photo ©1991 by John Dugdale. Reproduced by permission of Farrar, Straus & Giroux, Inc.; page 27: Cover from *The Handmaid's Tale* by Margaret Atwood. Jacket illustration/design ©1985 by Fred Marcellino. ©1985 by O.W. Toad Ltd. Reprinted by permission of Houghton Mifflin Company. All rights reserved; page 29: Cover reprinted by permission of the Putnam Publishing Group from *Stranger in a Strange Land* by Robert A. Heinlein. ©1961 by Robert A. Heinlein, renewed 1989, 1991 by Virginia Heinlein; page 29: Cover from *Alfred Hitchcock Presents: Stories That Go Bump in the Night.* ©1977. Reprinted with permission of Random House; page 29: Cover from *Love in the Time of Cholera* by Gabriel Garcia Marquez. Reprinted with permission of Alfred A. Knopf; page 29: Cover from *50 Simple Things You Can Do to Save the Earth.* Reprinted with permission of the EarthWorks Group; page 29: Cover from *Burnmarks* by Sara Paretsky. Used by permission of Dell Books, a division of Bantam Doubleday Dell Publishing Group, Inc.; page 29: Cover from *Totto-Chan: The Little Girl at the Window* by Tetsuko Kuroyanagi. Published by Kodansha International, Ltd. ©1981 by Tetsuko Kuroyanagi. English translation ©1982 by Kodansha International Ltd. Reprinted by permission. All rights reserved; page 40: Adapted from *"Rate Your Fitness Level,"* by Carl Sherman. Reprinted by permission of the author; page 30: Jacket copy adaptation reprinted by permission of the Putnam Publishing Group from *The Joy Luck Club* by Amy Tan. ©1989 by Amy Tan; page 30: Jacket copy adaptation reprinted by permission of the Putnam Publishing Group from *Stranger in a Strange Land* by Robert A. Heinlein. ©1961 by Robert A. Heinlein, renewed 1989, 1991 by Virginia Heinlein. Page 90: "What Kind of Job Is Best for You" © 1983 Singer Media Corporation, Seaview Business Park, 1030 Calle Cordillera, Unit 106, San Clemente, CA 92673. Reprinted from the December, 1983 issue of *Complete Woman*; page 91: "Personal Strategies to Prevent Backaches" reprinted by permission of Sales & Marketing Management, copyright May, 1992; page 110: "How To Reduce Stress and Be Happy on the Job" appeared in the November, 1982 issue of *The Miami Herald . . .* ©1982 *The Miami Herald.* Reprinted with permission; page 120: "If I Had A Hammer" (The Hammer Song). Words and music by Lee Hays and Pete Seeger. TRO © Copyright 1958 (Renewed) and 1962 (Renewed). Ludlow Music, Inc. New York, N.Y. Used by permission; page 120: Adaptation from *A Folk Song History of America* by Samuel L. Forcucci, ©1984. Reprinted by permission of the publisher, Prentice Hall/A Division of Simon & Schuster, Englewood Cliffs, N.J.; page 143: From *The Great American Bathroom Book.* Reprinted with permission of Compact Classics, Inc. ©1992; page 155: *Perplexing Puzzles and Tantalizing Teasers* copyright ©1969 by Martin Gardner. Reprinted by permission; page 155: From the book SUPERPUZZLES by Jean-Claude Baillif ©1982. Used by permission of the publisher, Prentice Hall/A Division of Simon & Schuster, Englewood Cliffs, N.J.; page 156: "Chronic Lateness: Learning to Leave It Behind" by Diane Cole. Courtesy of *Mademoiselle.* Copyright ©1981 by The Conde Nast Publications Inc.

The editors have made every effort to trace the ownership of all copyrighted material and express regret in advance for any error or omission. After notification of an oversight, they will include proper acknowledgment in future printings.